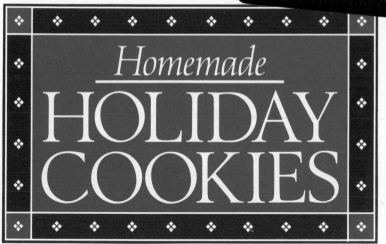

Homemade
HOLIDAY COOKIES

Homespun Holiday Favorites

Baking a batch of these delightful cookies will fill your home with holiday cheer.

GLAZED SUGAR COOKIES

COOKIES
- 1 package DUNCAN HINES® Golden Sugar Cookie Mix
- 1 egg

GLAZE
- 1 cup sifted confectioners sugar
- 1 to 2 tablespoons water or milk
- ½ teaspoon vanilla extract
- Food coloring (optional)
- Red and green sugar crystals, nonpareils or cinnamon candies

1. Preheat oven to 375°F.

2. **For cookies,** combine cookie mix, contents of buttery flavor packet from Mix and egg in large bowl. Stir until thoroughly blended. Roll dough to ⅛-inch thickness on lightly floured surface. Cut dough into desired shapes using floured cookie cutters. Place cookies 2 inches apart on ungreased baking sheets. Bake at 375°F for 5 to 6 minutes or until edges are light golden brown. Cool 1 minute on baking sheets. Remove to cooling racks. Cool completely.

3. **For glaze,** combine confectioners sugar, water and vanilla extract in small bowl. Beat until smooth. Tint glaze with food coloring, if desired. Brush glaze on each cookie with clean pastry brush. Sprinkle cookies with sugar crystals, nonpareils or cinnamon candies before glaze sets. Allow glaze to set before storing between layers of waxed paper in airtight container.   *Makes 2½ to 3 dozen cookies*

Glazed Sugar Cookies

SUGAR COOKIE WREATHS

1 package DUNCAN HINES®
   Golden Sugar Cookie Mix
1 egg

Green food coloring
Candied or maraschino
   cherry pieces

1. Preheat oven to 375°F. Combine cookie mix, contents of buttery flavor packet from Mix and egg in large bowl. Stir until thoroughly blended.

2. Tint dough with green food coloring. Stir until desired color. Form into balls the size of miniature marshmallows. For each wreath, arrange 9 or 10 balls with sides touching into a ring, 2 inches apart, on ungreased baking sheets. Flatten slightly with fingers. Place small piece of candied cherry on each ball.

3. Bake at 375°F for 5 to 7 minutes or until set but not browned. Cool 1 minute on baking sheets. Remove to cooling racks. Cool completely. Store in airtight container. *Makes 2 dozen cookies*

STAINED GLASS COOKIES

½ cup BLUE BONNET®
   Margarine, softened
½ cup sugar
½ cup honey
1 egg
1 teaspoon vanilla extract
3 cups all-purpose flour

1 teaspoon DAVIS® Baking
   Powder
½ teaspoon baking soda
½ teaspoon salt
5 rolls LIFE SAVERS® Fancy
   Fruits Candy

In large bowl with electric mixer at medium speed, beat margarine, sugar, honey, egg and vanilla extract until thoroughly blended. Blend in flour, baking powder, baking soda and salt. Cover; chill at least 2 hours.

On lightly floured surface, roll out dough to ¼-inch thickness. Cut dough with cookie cutters into desired shapes. Trace smaller version of cookie shape on dough leaving a ½- to ¾-inch border of dough. Cut out and remove dough from center of cookies. Place cookie outlines on baking sheets lined with foil.

Crush each color of candy separately between two layers of waxed paper with mallet. Spoon crushed candy inside centers of cookies.

Bake at 350°F for 6 to 8 minutes or until candy is melted and cookie is lightly browned. Cool cookies completely before removing from foil.
Makes 3½ dozen cookies

Sugar Cookie Wreaths

MERRY SPRITZ COOKIES

1 foil-wrapped bar
   (2 ounces) NESTLÉ®
   Premier White®
   baking bar
3/4 cup (1 1/2 sticks) butter or
   margarine, softened
1/2 cup sugar
1/2 teaspoon salt

1 egg
2 teaspoons vanilla extract
2 1/2 cups all-purpose flour
One 9-ounce package (1 1/2 cups)
   NESTLÉ® Toll House®
   semi-sweet chocolate
   Merry Morsels®

Preheat oven to 350°F. In small saucepan over low heat, melt Nestlé Premier White baking bar; set aside.

In large mixer bowl, beat butter, sugar and salt until creamy. Blend in egg and vanilla extract. Blend in melted baking bar. Gradually beat in flour. Place dough in cookie press fitted with desired plate. Press dough onto ungreased cookie sheets; decorate with Nestlé Toll House semi-sweet chocolate Merry Morsels.

Bake 7 to 9 minutes until set. Let stand 1 minute. Remove from cookie sheets; cool completely. *Makes about 6 dozen cookies*

CHOCOLATE-RASPBERRY SPRITZ

1 1/2 foil-wrapped bars
   (3 ounces) NESTLÉ®
   unsweetened chocolate
   baking bars
3/4 cup (1 1/2 sticks) butter or
   margarine, softened
1 cup sugar
1/2 teaspoon salt

1 egg
1/2 cup raspberry preserves
1 teaspoon vanilla extract
3 cups all-purpose flour
One 9-ounce package (1 1/2 cups)
   NESTLÉ® Toll House®
   semi-sweet chocolate
   Merry Morsels®

Preheat oven to 350°F. In small saucepan over low heat, melt Nestlé unsweetened chocolate baking bars; set aside.

In large mixer bowl, beat butter, sugar and salt until creamy. Blend in egg, preserves and vanilla extract. Blend in melted chocolate. Gradually beat in flour. Place dough in cookie press fitted with desired plate. Press dough onto ungreased cookie sheets; decorate with Nestlé Toll House semi-sweet chocolate Merry Morsels.

Bake 8 to 10 minutes until set. Let stand 1 minute. Remove from cookie sheets; cool completely. *Makes 8 dozen cookies*

Merry Spritz Cookies and Chocolate-Raspberry Spritz

YULETIDE GINGER COOKIES

¾ cup firmly packed brown
sugar
½ cup light corn syrup
½ cup (1 stick) margarine,
softened
2 egg whites, slightly beaten
3 cups QUAKER® Oat Bran
Hot Cereal, uncooked

¾ cup all-purpose flour
2 teaspoons ground ginger
1 teaspoon baking soda
1 teaspoon ground
cinnamon
¼ cup red or green colored
sugar crystals

Heat oven to 350°F. Beat brown sugar, corn syrup and margarine in large
bowl until fluffy. Blend in egg whites. Gradually add combined oat bran,
flour, ginger, baking soda and cinnamon; mix well. Shape into 1-inch
balls; roll in colored sugar crystals to coat. Place 2 inches apart on
ungreased cookie sheet. Gently press balls into 2-inch circles. Bake 11 to
13 minutes or until light golden brown. Cool 2 minutes on cookie sheet;
remove to wire rack. Cool completely. Store tightly covered.

Makes about 3½ dozen cookies

ANISE PILLOWS
PFEFFERNEUSSE

1²/₃ cups all-purpose flour
1¹/₂ teaspoons DAVIS® Baking
Powder
¹/₂ teaspoon grated lemon
peel
¹/₄ teaspoon salt
¹/₄ teaspoon ground
cinnamon
¹/₄ teaspoon ground nutmeg
¹/₈ teaspoon ground cloves

¹/₈ teaspoon white pepper
¹/₃ cup BLUE BONNET®
Margarine, softened
¹/₂ cup sugar
1 egg
¹/₂ cup milk
¹/₂ cup PLANTERS® Walnuts,
finely chopped
¹/₂ teaspoon anise seed
Confectioner's sugar

In small bowl, combine flour, baking powder, lemon peel, salt, spices and pepper; set aside. In large bowl, beat together margarine and sugar until creamy; beat in egg. Add flour mixture alternately with milk, beating well after each addition. Stir in walnuts and anise seed. Drop dough by teaspoonfuls, 2 inches apart, on lightly greased baking sheets.

Bake at 350°F for 15 to 17 minutes. Cool slightly on wire racks. Roll in confectioner's sugar while still warm; cool completely.

Makes 5 dozen cookies

OATMEAL-BANANA LEBKUCHEN

³/₄ cup margarine, softened
¹/₂ cup brown sugar, packed
¹/₄ cup honey
1¹/₂ teaspoons ground
cinnamon
1¹/₂ teaspoons ground ginger
1 teaspoon ground
cardamom
¹/₂ teaspoon ground cloves
2 extra-ripe, medium DOLE®
Bananas, peeled

2 eggs, beaten
1³/₄ cups all-purpose flour
¹/₂ teaspoon baking powder
¹/₂ teaspoon baking soda
¹/₂ teaspoon salt
³/₄ cup DOLE® Chopped
Almonds
¹/₂ cup mixed candied fruit,
finely chopped
2 cups quick oats, uncooked

LEMON GLAZE
³/₄ cup sifted powdered sugar
Juice from 1 DOLE® Lemon
(1 tablespoon)

1 drop almond extract

Continued

• Beat margarine, brown sugar and honey in large bowl. Beat in cinnamon, ginger, cardamom and cloves.

• Mash bananas with fork in small bowl; use 1 cup for recipe. Add 1 cup banana and eggs to margarine mixture; beat until blended.

• Combine flour, baking powder, baking soda and salt in small bowl. Stir in almonds and candied fruit. Add to margarine mixture. Stir until well blended. Stir in oats.

• Drop by heaping teaspoonfuls, 2 inches apart, onto greased cookie sheets. Bake in 400°F oven 8 minutes. Cool completely on wire racks. Spread with Lemon Glaze or dust with powdered sugar. When glaze has set, store cookies in airtight container.   *Makes 4 dozen cookies*

Lemon Glaze: Combine all ingredients until blended.

CHRISTMAS TREASURE NUGGETS

1 cup (2 sticks) margarine or
    butter, softened
1 cup firmly packed brown
    sugar
¾ cup granulated sugar
2 eggs
1 teaspoon vanilla
1¾ cups all-purpose flour
1 teaspoon baking soda

½ teaspoon baking powder
½ teaspoon salt (optional)
2 cups QUAKER® Oats (quick
    or old fashioned,
    uncooked)
2 cups QUAKER® 100%
    Natural Cereal, any
    flavor
Whole blanched almonds

Heat oven to 375°F. Beat margarine and sugars in large bowl until fluffy. Blend in eggs and vanilla. Combine flour, baking soda, baking powder and salt; add to margarine mixture and mix well. Stir in oats and cereal.

Drop by rounded teaspoonfuls, 2 inches apart, onto ungreased cookie sheet. Press 1 almond onto each cookie. Bake 8 to 10 minutes or until golden brown. Cool 2 minutes on cookie sheet; remove to wire rack. Cool completely. Store tightly covered.   *Makes 6 dozen cookies*

Milk Chocolate Florentine Cookies

MILK CHOCOLATE FLORENTINE COOKIES

^{2}/₃ cup butter or margarine
2 cups quick oats, uncooked
1 cup sugar
^{2}/₃ cup all-purpose flour
^{1}/₄ cup corn syrup
^{1}/₄ cup milk

1 teaspoon vanilla extract
^{1}/₄ teaspoon salt
One 11^1/₂-ounce package
(2 cups) NESTLÉ® Toll
House® milk chocolate
morsels

Preheat oven to 375°F.

Melt butter in medium saucepan over low heat. Remove from heat. Stir in oats, sugar, flour, corn syrup, milk, vanilla extract and salt; mix well. Drop by measuring teaspoonfuls, about 3 inches apart, onto foil-lined cookie sheets. Spread thin with rubber spatula.

Bake 5 to 7 minutes. Cool on cookie sheets. Peel foil away from cookies.

Melt Nestlé Toll House milk chocolate morsels over hot (not boiling) water; stir until smooth. Spread chocolate on flat side of half the cookies. Top with remaining cookies.   *Makes 3^1/₂ dozen sandwich cookies*

SUGAR COOKIE ORNAMENTS

1 package DUNCAN HINES®
   Golden Sugar Cookie Mix
1 egg
1 teaspoon milk
   Assorted colored sugar
   crystals, cinnamon
   gems, nonpareils or
   decors

DUNCAN HINES® Vanilla
Layer Cake Frosting
(optional)

1. Preheat oven to 375°F.

2. Combine cookie mix, contents of buttery flavor packet from Mix, egg
and milk in large bowl. Stir until thoroughly blended. Form dough into
1-inch balls. Place 3 inches apart on ungreased baking sheets. Grease and
flour bottom of drinking glass. Press gently to flatten cookies to form
2-inch circles.

3. Press end of drinking straw into top of each cookie to make hole.
Decorate cookies as desired or leave plain to frost.

4. Bake at 375°F for 5 to 7 minutes or until set but not browned. Press
straw through holes in top of cookies again. Cool 1 minute on baking
sheets. Remove to cooling racks. Cool completely. Frost plain cookies, if
desired.

5. String ribbon through holes in cookies. Tie at top.

Makes 3½ to 4 dozen cookies

Tip: Frosting can be divided and tinted with a few drops of red and green
food coloring. Stir until well blended. Frost patterns on ornaments or
frost and sprinkle with decors.

Painted Ornaments: Combine 1 egg yolk and 1 teaspoon water. Stir
well. Divide into 3 custard cups. Tint each with 1 drop of different food
coloring. Sketch design on unbaked cookie with tip of knife. Use clean
watercolor paint brushes to paint designs on cookies before baking. Bake
and cool as directed.

PREMIER WHITE® SUGAR COOKIES

Two 6-ounce packages (6 foil-
   wrapped bars) NESTLÉ®
   Premier White® baking
   bars, divided
2¼ cups all-purpose flour
   1 teaspoon baking powder
   ¼ teaspoon salt
   ½ cup (1 stick) butter or
   margarine, softened

⅓ cup sugar
1 egg
1 teaspoon vanilla extract
One 9-ounce package (1½ cups)
   NESTLÉ® Toll House®
   semi-sweet chocolate
   Merry Morsels®

Preheat oven to 350°F. In small saucepan over low heat, melt 3 foil-
wrapped bars (6 ounces) Nestlé Premier White baking bars; set aside. In
small bowl, combine flour, baking powder and salt; set aside.

In large mixer bowl, beat butter and sugar until creamy. Blend in egg and
vanilla extract. Beat in melted baking bars. Gradually beat in flour
mixture until soft dough forms. Shape dough into ball; flatten to ¾-inch
thickness. Wrap in plastic wrap; refrigerate 15 minutes until firm.

On lightly floured surface, roll out dough to ⅛-inch thickness. With 2½-
to 3-inch cookie cutters, cut dough into shapes. Place on ungreased
cookie sheets.

Bake 8 to 10 minutes until edges are golden brown. Let stand 2 minutes.
Remove from cookie sheets; cool completely.

In small saucepan over low heat, melt remaining 3 foil-wrapped bars
(6 ounces) baking bars. Spread or pipe melted baking bars on cookies.
Decorate with Nestlé Toll House semi-sweet chocolate Merry Morsels,
attaching with melted baking bars.   *Makes about 3½ dozen cookies*

Christmas Tree Hanging Cookies: With skewer, make ½-inch hole near
top edge of each cutout before baking.

Premier White® Sugar Cookies

HOLIDAY ALMOND WREATHS

¾ cup FLEISCHMANN'S®
   Margarine, softened
½ cup sugar
¼ cup EGG BEATERS®
   Cholesterol-Free 99%
   Real Egg Product, thawed

1 teaspoon almond extract
2 cups all-purpose flour
½ cup ground PLANTERS®
   Almonds
   Green and red candied
   cherries (optional)

In medium bowl with electric mixer at medium speed, beat margarine and sugar until light and fluffy. Add egg product and almond extract; beat well. Stir in flour and ground almonds. Using pastry bag with ½-inch star tip, pipe dough into 1½-inch wreaths, 2 inches apart, on ungreased baking sheets. Decorate wreaths with green and red candied cherries, if desired. Bake at 400°F for 10 to 12 minutes or until golden brown. Cool on wire racks. *Makes 3 dozen cookies*

SUGAR COOKIES

1 cup BUTTER FLAVOR
   CRISCO®
1 cup sugar
1 egg
1½ teaspoons vanilla

2 cups all-purpose flour
1 teaspoon baking soda
1 teaspoon cream of tartar
½ teaspoon salt

1. Cream Butter Flavor Crisco and sugar in large bowl at medium speed of electric mixer. Beat in egg and vanilla.

2. Combine flour with baking soda, cream of tartar and salt. Blend into creamed mixture. Cover and chill at least 2 hours.

3. Preheat oven to 375°F.

4. Roll out dough on floured surface to ⅛-inch thickness. Cut into desired shapes with cookie cutters. Place on ungreased baking sheets.

5. Bake at 375°F for 6 to 7 minutes. Cool on baking sheets about 1 minute. Remove to cooling racks. *Makes 5½ to 6 dozen cookies*

Note: For holidays, cut dough into desired holiday shapes. Sprinkle with colored sugar crystals before baking.

LINZER TARTS

1 cup BLUE BONNET®
  Margarine, softened
1 cup granulated sugar
2 cups all-purpose flour
1 cup PLANTERS® Slivered
  Almonds, chopped

1 teaspoon grated lemon
  peel
1/4 teaspoon ground
  cinnamon
1/3 cup raspberry preserves
  Confectioner's sugar

In large bowl with electric mixer at high speed, beat margarine and granulated sugar until light and fluffy. Stir in flour, almonds, lemon peel and cinnamon until blended. Cover; chill 2 hours.

Divide dough in half. On floured surface, roll out one half of dough to 1/8-inch thickness. Using 2 1/2-inch round cookie cutter, cut circles from dough. Reroll scraps to make additional rounds. Cut out 1/2-inch circles from centers of half the rounds. Repeat with remaining dough. Place on ungreased baking sheets. Bake at 325°F for 12 to 15 minutes or until lightly browned. Remove from sheets; cool on wire racks. Spread preserves on top of whole cookies. Top with cut-out cookies to make sandwiches. Dust with confectioner's sugar.   *Makes 2 dozen cookies*

GINGERBREAD COOKIES

1/2 cup vegetable shortening
1/3 cup packed light brown
  sugar
1/4 cup dark molasses
1 egg white
1/2 teaspoon vanilla
1 1/2 cups all-purpose flour

1/2 teaspoon baking soda
1/4 teaspoon baking powder
1/2 teaspoon salt
1 teaspoon ground
  cinnamon
1/2 teaspoon ground ginger

Beat shortening, brown sugar, molasses, egg white and vanilla in large bowl at high speed of electric mixer until smooth. Combine flour, baking soda, baking powder, salt and spices in small bowl. Add to shortening mixture; mix well. Cover; refrigerate until firm, about 8 hours or overnight.

Preheat oven to 350°F. Grease cookie sheets. Roll out dough on lightly floured surface to 1/8-inch thickness. Cut into desired shapes with cookie cutters. Place on prepared cookie sheets.

Bake 6 to 8 minutes or until edges begin to brown. Remove to wire racks; cool completely. Decorate as desired.   *Makes about 2 1/2 dozen cookies*

SPICED BANANA COOKIE WREATHS

2 extra-ripe, medium DOLE®
   Bananas, peeled
2 cups granola
1½ cups all-purpose flour
1 cup brown sugar, packed
1 teaspoon baking powder
1 teaspoon ground
   cinnamon
½ teaspoon ground nutmeg
¼ teaspoon salt
1 egg

½ cup margarine, melted
¼ cup vegetable oil
1 cup DOLE® Raisins
⅓ cup chopped DOLE®
   Almonds
½ cup powdered sugar
1 tablespoon milk
Candied cherries or
   colored sugar crystals
   (optional)

• Place bananas in blender. Process until puréed; use 1 cup for recipe.

• Combine granola, flour, brown sugar, baking powder, cinnamon, nutmeg and salt in large bowl. Beat in 1 cup banana, egg, margarine and oil. Stir in raisins. For each of 3 wreaths, arrange about 16 generous teaspoonfuls dough with sides touching into a ring on greased cookie sheets. Sprinkle with almonds.

• Bake in 375°F oven 15 to 18 minutes until lightly browned. Cool on baking sheets.

• Combine powdered sugar and milk in small bowl until smooth. Drizzle over cooled wreaths. Decorate with candied cherries if desired. Tie with a bow to give as a gift.   *Makes 3 wreaths (16 cookies per wreath)*

SNOW-COVERED ALMOND CRESCENTS

1 cup (2 sticks) margarine or
   butter, softened
¾ cup powdered sugar
½ teaspoon almond extract
   or 2 teaspoons vanilla
   extract
2 cups all-purpose flour

¼ teaspoon salt (optional)
1 cup QUAKER® Oats (quick
   or old fashioned,
   uncooked)
½ cup finely chopped
   almonds
Additional powdered sugar

Heat oven to 325°F. Beat margarine, powdered sugar and almond extract until fluffy. Add flour and salt; mix until well blended. Stir in oats and almonds. Using level measuring tablespoonfuls, shape dough into crescents. Bake on ungreased cookie sheet 14 to 17 minutes or until bottoms are light golden brown. Remove to wire rack. Sift additional powdered sugar generously over warm cookies. Cool completely.

Makes about 4 dozen cookies

RICHEST SPRITZ

1¼ cups confectioners' sugar
1 cup butter, softened
2 egg yolks *or* 1 whole egg
1 teaspoon vanilla extract

½ teaspoon almond extract (optional)
2½ cups all-purpose flour
½ teaspoon salt
Food color (optional)

Preheat oven to 400°F. Cream confectioners' sugar and butter in large bowl with electric mixer at medium speed. Beat in egg yolks, vanilla and almond extracts. Combine flour and salt. Add to butter mixture; mix well. Tint dough with food color, if desired. Place dough in cookie press fitted with plate. Load press with dough. Press onto ungreased cookie sheets, about 2 inches apart. Decorate as desired. Bake 6 to 8 minutes or until very slightly browned around edges. Remove to wire racks to cool.

Makes about 6½ dozen cookies

Spiced Banana Cookie Wreath

PEANUT BUTTER REINDEER

COOKIES

1 package DUNCAN HINES®
    Peanut Butter
    Cookie Mix

1 egg
2 teaspoons all-purpose
    flour

ASSORTED DECORATIONS

Miniature semi-sweet
    chocolate chips
Vanilla milk chips

Candy-coated semi-sweet
    chocolate chips
Colored sprinkles

1. **For cookies,** combine cookie mix, contents of peanut butter packet from Mix and egg in large bowl. Stir until thoroughly blended. Form dough into ball. Place flour in jumbo (15×13-inch) resealable plastic bag. Place ball of dough in bag. Shake to coat with flour. Place dough in center of bag (do not seal). Roll dough with rolling pin out to edges of bag. Slide bag onto baking sheet. Chill in refrigerator at least 1 hour.

2. Preheat oven to 375°F. Use scissors to cut bag down center and across ends. Turn plastic back to uncover dough. Dip reindeer cookie cutter in flour. Cut dough with reindeer cookie cutter. Dip cookie cutter in flour after each cut. Transfer cut-out cookies to ungreased baking sheets using floured pancake turner. Decorate each reindeer as desired. Bake at 375°F for 5 to 7 minutes or until set but not browned. Cool 2 minutes on baking sheets. Remove to cooling racks. Cool completely. Store between layers of waxed paper in airtight container.   *Makes about 2 dozen cookies*

Tip: Reroll dough by folding plastic back over dough.

SANTA'S THUMBPRINTS

1 cup (2 sticks) margarine,
    softened
½ cup firmly packed brown
    sugar
1 whole egg or egg white
1 teaspoon vanilla

1½ cups QUAKER® Oats (quick
    or old fashioned,
    uncooked)
1½ cups all-purpose flour
1 cup finely chopped nuts
⅓ cup jelly or preserves

Heat oven to 350°F. Beat margarine and sugar in large bowl until fluffy. Blend in egg and vanilla. Add combined oats and flour; mix well. Shape into 1-inch balls; roll in chopped nuts. Place 2 inches apart on ungreased cookie sheet. Make indentation in center of each ball with thumb. Fill each thumbprint with about ¼ teaspoon jelly. Bake 12 to 15 minutes or until light golden brown. Cool completely on wire rack. Store loosely covered.   *Makes about 3 dozen cookies*

Peanut Butter Reindeer

Chips 'n' Chocolate

Chocolate in every flavor and form is evident in this chapter—white, dark and milk chocolate in chips, glazes, fillings and more!

CHOCOLATE CHIPS THUMBPRINT COOKIES

1 cup HERSHEY'S Semi-Sweet
   Chocolate Chips, divided
¼ cup butter or margarine,
   softened
¼ cup shortening
½ cup sugar

1 egg, separated
½ teaspoon vanilla extract
1 cup all-purpose flour
¼ teaspoon salt
1 cup finely chopped nuts

Heat oven to 350°F. In small microwave-safe bowl, place ¼ cup chocolate chips. Microwave at HIGH (100%) 20 to 30 seconds or just until chocolate is melted and smooth when stirred; set aside to cool slightly. In large mixer bowl, combine butter, shortening, sugar, reserved melted chocolate, egg yolk and vanilla; blend well. Stir in flour and salt.
Roll dough into 1-inch balls. With fork, slightly beat egg white. Dip each ball into egg white; roll in chopped nuts. Place balls on ungreased cookie sheet, about 1 inch apart. Press center of each ball with thumb to make indentation. Bake 10 to 12 minutes or until set. Remove from oven; immediately place several of remaining ¾ cup chocolate chips in center of each cookie. Carefully remove from cookie sheet to wire rack. After several minutes, swirl melted chocolate in each thumbprint. Cool completely. *Makes about 2½ dozen cookies*

Chocolate Chips Thumbprint Cookies

White Chocolate Biggies and Peanut Butter Jumbos

WHITE CHOCOLATE BIGGIES

1½ cups butter or margarine, softened
1 cup granulated sugar
¾ cup packed light brown sugar
2 teaspoons vanilla
2 eggs
2½ cups all-purpose flour
⅔ cup unsweetened cocoa
1 teaspoon baking soda
½ teaspoon salt
1 package (10 ounces) large, white chocolate chips
¾ cup pecan halves, coarsely chopped
½ cup golden raisins

Preheat oven to 350°F. Lightly grease cookie sheets or line with parchment paper. Beat butter, sugars, vanilla and eggs in large bowl until light and fluffy. Combine flour, cocoa, baking soda and salt in medium bowl; blend into creamed mixture until smooth. Stir in white chocolate chips, pecans and raisins. Scoop out about ⅓ cup dough for each cookie. Place on prepared cookie sheets, about 4 inches apart. Flatten each cookie slightly. Bake 12 to 14 minutes or until firm in center. Cool 5 minutes on cookie sheets; remove to wire racks to cool completely.

Makes about 2 dozen large cookies

PEANUT BUTTER JUMBOS

1½ cups peanut butter
½ cup butter or margarine,
    softened
1 cup packed brown sugar
1 cup granulated sugar
3 eggs
2 tablespoons baking soda

1 teaspoon vanilla
4½ cups rolled oats, uncooked
1 cup (6 ounces) semisweet
    chocolate chips
1 cup candy-coated
    chocolate pieces

Preheat oven to 350°F. Lightly grease cookie sheets or line with
parchment paper. Beat peanut butter, butter, sugars and eggs in large
bowl until light and fluffy. Blend in baking soda, vanilla and oats until
well mixed. Stir in chocolate chips and candy pieces. Scoop out about ⅓
cup dough for each cookie. Place on prepared cookie sheets, about 4
inches apart. Flatten each cookie slightly. Bake 15 to 20 minutes or until
firm in center. Remove to wire racks to cool completely.

Makes about 1½ dozen large cookies

ALMOND DOUBLE CHIP COOKIES

¾ cup butter or margarine,
    softened
¾ cup packed light brown
    sugar
1 egg
½ teaspoon almond extract
1½ cups all-purpose flour
¼ teaspoon baking soda

Dash salt
1 cup (6 ounces) semisweet
    chocolate chips
1 cup (6 ounces) vanilla
    milk chips
½ cup slivered blanched
    almonds

Preheat oven to 375°F. Line cookie sheets with parchment paper or leave
ungreased. Beat butter and brown sugar in large bowl until creamy. Beat
in egg and almond extract. Combine flour, baking soda and salt in small
bowl. Blend into butter mixture. Stir in semisweet and vanilla milk chips
and almonds. Drop dough by rounded tablespoonfuls, 3 inches apart, onto
prepared cookie sheets. Bake 8 to 10 minutes or until light brown. *Do not
overbake.* Cool 2 minutes on cookie sheets; remove to wire racks to cool
completely.

Makes about 3 dozen cookies

ORIGINAL TOLL HOUSE® CHOCOLATE CHIP COOKIES

2¼ cups all-purpose flour
1 teaspoon baking soda
1 teaspoon salt
1 cup (2 sticks) butter, softened
¾ cup granulated sugar
¾ cup firmly packed brown sugar

2 eggs
1 teaspoon vanilla extract
One 12-ounce package (2 cups) NESTLE® Toll House® semi-sweet chocolate morsels
1 cup nuts, chopped

Preheat oven to 375°F. In small bowl, combine flour, baking soda and salt; set aside.

In large mixer bowl, beat butter, granulated sugar and brown sugar until creamy. Add eggs, 1 at a time, beating well after each addition. Blend in vanilla extract. Gradually beat in flour mixture. Stir in Nestlé Toll House semi-sweet chocolate morsels and nuts. Drop by rounded measuring tablespoonfuls onto ungreased cookie sheets.

Bake 9 to 11 minutes until edges are golden brown. Let stand 2 minutes. Remove from cookie sheets; cool completely.

Makes about 5 dozen cookies

Toll House Pan Cookies: Preheat oven to 375°F. Prepare dough as directed; spread in greased 15½ × 10½-inch baking pan. Bake 20 to 25 minutes until golden brown. Cool completely. Cut into 2-inch squares. Makes about 3 dozen cookies.

Refrigerator Toll House Cookies: Prepare dough as directed. Divide dough in half; wrap halves separately in waxed paper. Refrigerate 1 hour or until firm. On waxed paper, shape each dough half into 15-inch log; wrap in waxed paper. Refrigerate 30 minutes.*

Preheat oven to 375°F. Cut each log into 30 (½-inch) slices. Place on ungreased cookie sheets. Bake 8 to 10 minutes until edges are golden brown. Makes 5 dozen cookies.

*Dough may be stored up to 1 week in refrigerator or up to 8 weeks in freezer, if foil- or freezer-wrapped.

Original Toll House® Chocolate Chip Cookies

CHOCOLATE CHIP LOLLIPOPS

1 package DUNCAN HINES®
   Chocolate Chip
   Cookie Mix
1 egg

2 teaspoons water
24 flat ice cream sticks
Assorted decors

1. Preheat oven to 375°F.

2. Combine cookie mix, buttery flavor packet from Mix, egg and water in large bowl. Stir until thoroughly blended. Shape dough into 24 (1-inch) balls. Place balls 3 inches apart on ungreased baking sheets. Push ice cream stick into center of each ball. Flatten each ball with hand to form round lollipop. Decorate by pressing decors onto dough.

3. Bake at 375°F for 8 to 9 minutes or until light golden brown. Cool 1 minute on baking sheets. Remove to cooling racks. Cool completely. Store in airtight container. *Makes 2 dozen cookies*

Tip: For best results, use shiny baking sheets for baking cookies. Dark baking sheets cause cookie bottoms to become too brown.

MINT CHOCOLATE CHEWS

½ cup BLUE BONNET®
   Margarine
1 cup sugar
2 (1-ounce) squares
   unsweetened chocolate,
   melted
1 egg
⅓ cup buttermilk

1 teaspoon vanilla extract
1¾ cups all-purpose flour
½ teaspoon baking soda
¼ teaspoon salt
3 (.35-ounce) packages
   Pep-O-Mint LIFE SAVERS®
   Holes
½ cup walnuts, chopped

In large bowl with mixer at medium speed, beat margarine, sugar, melted chocolate and egg until creamy. Stir in buttermilk and vanilla until smooth. Mix in flour, baking soda and salt until blended; stir in holes and walnuts. Cover and chill dough at least 1 hour.

Drop dough by level tablespoonfuls, 2 inches apart, onto ungreased baking sheets. Bake at 400°F for 8 to 10 minutes or until set. Remove from sheets; cool on wire racks. *Makes 3 dozen cookies*

Chocolate Chip Lollipops

CHOCOLATE MINT PINWHEELS

One 10-ounce package
  (1½ cups) NESTLÉ® Toll
  House® mint flavored
  semi-sweet chocolate
  morsels, divided
¾ cup (1½ sticks) butter,
  softened

⅓ cup sugar
½ teaspoon salt
1 egg
1 teaspoon vanilla extract
2¼ cups all-purpose flour

Over hot (not boiling) water, melt ½ cup Nestlé Toll House mint flavored semi-sweet chocolate morsels, stirring until smooth. Cool to room temperature; set aside.

In large mixer bowl, beat butter, sugar and salt until creamy. Beat in egg and vanilla extract.* Gradually add flour.

Place 1 cup dough in medium bowl; blend in reserved melted morsels. Shape each dough into a ball; flatten and cover with plastic wrap. Refrigerate until firm, about 1½ hours.

Preheat oven to 375°F. Between sheets of waxed paper, roll each ball of dough into a 13×9-inch rectangle. Remove top layers of waxed paper. Invert chocolate dough onto plain dough. Peel off remaining waxed paper. Starting with a long side, roll up, jelly-roll style. Cut into ¼-inch slices; place on ungreased cookie sheets.

Bake 7 to 10 minutes. Let stand on cookie sheets 2 minutes. Remove from cookie sheets; cool completely.

Over hot (not boiling) water, melt remaining 1 cup mint flavored semi-sweet chocolate morsels, stirring until smooth. Spread flat side of each cookie with slightly rounded ½ teaspoonful melted chocolate. Refrigerate 10 minutes to set chocolate.   *Makes 3½ dozen cookies*

*Mixture may look curdled.

*Clockwise from top right: Chocolate Mint
Pinwheels; Chocolate Raspberry Linzer
Cookies (page 30); New Wave Chocolate Spritz
Cookies (page 30)*

CHOCOLATE RASPBERRY LINZER COOKIES

2⅓ cups all-purpose flour
1 teaspoon baking powder
½ teaspoon cinnamon
½ teaspoon salt
1 cup sugar
¾ cup (1½ sticks) butter, softened
2 eggs

½ teaspoon almond extract
One 12-ounce package (2 cups) NESTLÉ® Toll House® semi-sweet chocolate morsels
6 tablespoons raspberry jam or preserves
Confectioners' sugar

In small bowl, combine flour, baking powder, cinnamon and salt; set aside. In large mixer bowl, beat sugar and butter until creamy. Beat in eggs and almond extract. Gradually add flour mixture. Divide dough in half. Wrap in plastic wrap; refrigerate until firm.

Preheat oven to 350°F. On lightly floured board, roll out half of dough to ⅛-inch thickness. Cut with 2½-inch round cookie cutter. Repeat with remaining dough. Cut 1-inch-round centers from half of unbaked cookies. Place on ungreased cookie sheets. Reroll dough trimmings, if necessary.

Bake 8 to 10 minutes just until set. Let stand on cookie sheets 2 minutes. Remove from cookie sheets; cool completely.

Over hot (not boiling) water, melt Nestlé Toll House semi-sweet chocolate morsels, stirring until smooth. Spread 1 measuring teaspoonful melted chocolate on flat side of each whole cookie. Top with ½ measuring teaspoon raspberry jam. Sprinkle confectioners' sugar on cookies with center holes; place flat side down on top of chocolate-jam cookies to form cookie sandwiches.

Makes about 3 dozen sandwich cookies

NEW WAVE CHOCOLATE SPRITZ COOKIES

One 6-ounce package (1 cup) NESTLÉ® Toll House® semi-sweet chocolate morsels
1 cup (2 sticks) butter, softened

⅔ cup sugar
1 teaspoon vanilla extract
2 eggs
2½ cups all-purpose flour
One 4-ounce jar cinnamon candies

Continued

Over hot (not boiling) water, melt Nestlé Toll House semi-sweet chocolate morsels, stirring until smooth; set aside.

In large mixer bowl, beat butter, sugar and vanilla extract until creamy. Beat in eggs. Stir in melted morsels. Gradually beat in flour. Cover dough; refrigerate 30 to 45 minutes.

Preheat oven to 400°F. Place dough in cookie press fitted with star plate. Press dough into 2-inch circles on ungreased cookie sheets; decorate with cinnamon candies.

Bake 5 minutes or just until set. Let stand on cookie sheets 2 minutes. Remove from cookie sheets; cool completely.

Makes about 7½ dozen cookies

CHOCOLATE MINT SNOW-TOP COOKIES

1½ cups all-purpose flour
1½ teaspoons baking powder
¼ teaspoon salt
One 10-ounce package
    (1½ cups) NESTLÉ® Toll
    House® mint flavored
    semi-sweet chocolate
    morsels, divided

6 tablespoons (¾ stick)
    butter, softened
1 cup granulated sugar
1½ teaspoons vanilla extract
2 eggs
    Confectioners' sugar

In small bowl, combine flour, baking powder and salt; set aside. Over hot (not boiling) water, melt 1 cup Nestlé Toll House mint flavored semi-sweet chocolate morsels, stirring until smooth; set aside.

In large mixer bowl, beat butter and granulated sugar until creamy. Add melted mint flavored semi-sweet chocolate morsels and vanilla extract. Beat in eggs. Gradually beat in flour mixture. Stir in remaining ½ cup mint flavored semi-sweet chocolate morsels. Wrap dough in plastic wrap and freeze until firm, about 20 minutes.

Preheat oven to 350°F. Shape dough into 1-inch balls; coat with confectioners' sugar. Place on ungreased cookie sheets.

Bake 10 to 12 minutes until tops appear cracked. Let stand on cookie sheets 5 minutes. Remove from cookie sheets; cool completely.

Makes about 3 dozen cookies

CHOCOLATE SUGAR COOKIES

3 squares BAKER'S®
   Unsweetened Chocolate
1 cup (2 sticks) margarine or
   butter
1 cup sugar
1 egg

1 teaspoon vanilla
2 cups all-purpose flour
1 teaspoon baking soda
1/4 teaspoon salt
   Additional sugar

Microwave chocolate and margarine in large microwavable bowl on HIGH 2 minutes or until margarine is melted. Stir until chocolate is completely melted.

Stir 1 cup sugar into melted chocolate mixture until well blended. Stir in egg and vanilla until completely blended. Mix in flour, baking soda and salt. Refrigerate 30 minutes.

Heat oven to 375°F. Shape dough into 1-inch balls; roll in additional sugar. Place, 2 inches apart, on ungreased cookie sheets. (If flatter, crisper cookies are desired, flatten balls with bottom of drinking glass.)

Bake 8 to 10 minutes or until set. Remove from cookie sheets to cool on wire racks. *Makes about 3½ dozen cookies*

Prep time: 15 minutes
Chill time: 30 minutes
Baking time: 8 to 10 minutes

Jam-Filled Chocolate Sugar Cookies: Prepare Chocolate Sugar Cookie dough as directed. Roll in finely chopped nuts in place of sugar. Make indentation in each ball; fill center with your favorite jam. Bake as directed.

Chocolate-Caramel Sugar Cookies: Prepare Chocolate Sugar Cookie dough as directed. Roll in finely chopped nuts in place of sugar. Make indentation in each ball; bake as directed. Microwave 1 package (14 ounces) KRAFT Caramels with 2 tablespoons milk in microwavable bowl on HIGH 3 minutes or until melted, stirring after 2 minutes. Fill centers of cookies with caramel mixture. Drizzle with melted BAKER'S Semi-Sweet Chocolate.

Top to bottom: Chocolate Sugar Cookies; Jam-Filled Chocolate Sugar Cookies; Chocolate-Caramel Sugar Cookies

CHOCOLATE MELTING MOMENTS

1 cup butter or margarine,
    softened
1/3 cup confectioners sugar
1/4 cup unsweetened cocoa

1 1/2 cups cake flour
    Mocha Filling (recipe
    follows)

Preheat oven to 350°F. Lightly grease cookie sheets or line with
parchment paper. Beat 1 cup butter, confectioners sugar and cocoa in
large bowl until fluffy. Blend in cake flour until smooth. Shape dough
into marble-size balls. (If dough is too soft to handle, cover and
refrigerate until firm.) Place 2 inches apart on prepared cookie sheets.
Press center of each ball with knuckle of finger to make indentation.
Bake 10 to 12 minutes or until set. Remove to wire racks. Prepare Mocha
Filling. While cookies are still warm, spoon about 1/2 teaspoonful filling
into center of each.   *Makes about 5 dozen cookies*

MOCHA FILLING

1 tablespoon butter or
    margarine
1 square (1 ounce)
    unsweetened chocolate

1 cup confectioners sugar
1 teaspoon vanilla
1 to 2 tablespoons hot coffee
    or water

Melt 1 tablespoon butter and chocolate in small heavy saucepan over low
heat; stir until melted. Blend in confectioners sugar, vanilla and enough
coffee to make a smooth filling.

ALL-AMERICAN CHOCOLATE CHIP COOKIES

2/3 cup butter or margarine,
    softened
1/3 cup shortening
1 cup packed brown sugar
1/2 cup granulated sugar
1 egg
1 teaspoon vanilla

2 cups all-purpose flour
1 teaspoon baking soda
1 teaspoon salt
1 package (12 ounces)
    semisweet chocolate
    chips
1 cup chopped walnuts

In large bowl, cream butter, shortening and sugars. Beat in egg and
vanilla. Combine flour, baking soda and salt; stir into butter mixture,
mixing well. Stir in chocolate chips and nuts. Drop by teaspoonfuls, 2
inches apart, onto greased baking sheets. Bake in 350°F oven 8 to 10
minutes, just until edges are golden (centers will still be soft). Remove to
wire racks to cool.   *Makes about 3 dozen cookies*

Favorite recipe from Walnut Marketing Board

CHOCOLATE MINT SUGAR COOKIE DROPS

2½ cups all-purpose flour
1¼ teaspoons baking powder
¾ teaspoon salt
1 cup granulated sugar
¾ cup vegetable oil
2 eggs
1 teaspoon vanilla extract

One 10-ounce package
(1½ cups) NESTLÉ® Toll
House® mint flavored
semi-sweet chocolate
morsels
Assorted colored sugars or
additional granulated
sugar

Preheat oven to 350°F. In small bowl, combine flour, baking powder and salt; set aside.

In large mixer bowl, combine granulated sugar and oil. Add eggs, 1 at a time, beating well after each addition. Blend in vanilla extract. Gradually beat in flour mixture. Stir in Nestlé Toll House mint flavored semi-sweet chocolate morsels. Shape rounded measuring teaspoonfuls of dough into balls; roll in colored sugar. Place on ungreased cookie sheets.

Bake 8 to 10 minutes until set. Let stand on cookie sheets 2 minutes. Remove from cookie sheets; cool completely.

Makes about 5½ dozen cookies

Chocolate Mint Sugar Cookie Drops

CHOCOLATE LACE CORNUCOPIAS

½ cup firmly packed brown
    sugar
½ cup corn syrup
¼ cup (½ stick) margarine or
    butter
 4 squares BAKER'S® Semi-
    Sweet Chocolate

1 cup all-purpose flour
1 cup finely chopped nuts
    Whipped cream or COOL
    WHIP® Whipped
    Topping, thawed

Heat oven to 350°F. Microwave sugar, corn syrup and margarine in large
microwavable bowl on HIGH 2 minutes or until boiling. Stir in chocolate
until completely melted. Gradually stir in flour and nuts until well
blended. Drop by level tablespoonfuls, 4 inches apart, onto foil-lined
cookie sheets.

Bake 10 minutes. Lift foil and cookies onto wire racks. Cool 3 to 4
minutes or until cookies can be easily peeled off foil. Remove foil; finish
cooling cookies on wire racks that have been covered with paper towels.

Place several cookies, lacy side down, on foil-lined cookie sheet. Heat at
350°F for 2 to 3 minutes or until slightly softened. Remove from foil, 1 at
a time, and roll, lacy side out, to form cones. Cool completely. Just before
serving, fill with whipped cream.   *Makes about 30 cornucopias*

Prep time: 20 minutes
Baking time: 12 to 13 minutes

Saucepan preparation: Mix sugar, corn syrup and margarine in 2-quart
saucepan. Bring to boil over medium heat, stirring constantly. Remove
from heat; stir in chocolate until completely melted. Continue as directed.

Chocolate Lace Cornucopias

Peanut Butter and Chocolate Cookie Sandwich Cookies

PEANUT BUTTER AND CHOCOLATE COOKIE SANDWICH COOKIES

½ cup REESE'S Peanut Butter Chips
3 tablespoons plus ½ cup butter or margarine, softened and divided
1¼ cups sugar, divided
¼ cup light corn syrup
1 egg
1 teaspoon vanilla extract
2 cups plus 2 tablespoons all-purpose flour, divided

2 teaspoons baking soda
¼ teaspoon salt
½ cup HERSHEY'S Cocoa
5 tablespoons butter or margarine, melted
Additional sugar
About 2 dozen large marshmallows

Continued

38

Heat oven to 350°F. In small saucepan over very low heat, melt peanut butter chips and 3 tablespoons softened butter. Remove from heat; cool slightly. In large mixer bowl, beat remaining ½ cup softened butter and 1 cup sugar until light and fluffy. Add corn syrup, egg and vanilla; blend thoroughly. Combine 2 cups flour, baking soda and salt; add to butter mixture, blending well. Remove 1¼ cups batter and place in small bowl; with wooden spoon, stir in remaining 2 tablespoons flour and peanut butter chip mixture. Blend cocoa, remaining ¼ cup sugar and melted butter into remaining batter. Refrigerate both batters 5 to 10 minutes or until firm enough to handle.

Roll both doughs into 1-inch balls; roll in additional sugar. Place on ungreased cookie sheet. Bake 10 to 11 minutes or until set. Cool slightly; remove from cookie sheet to wire rack. Cool completely. Place 1 marshmallow on flat side of 1 chocolate cookie. Microwave at MEDIUM (50%) 10 seconds or until marshmallow is softened; place a peanut butter cookie over marshmallow, pressing down slightly. Repeat with remaining marshmallows and cookies. Serve immediately.

Makes about 2 dozen sandwich cookies

NUTTY CHOCOLATE STARS

¾ cup (1½ sticks) margarine
  or butter, softened
¾ cup firmly packed brown
  sugar
1 egg
1 teaspoon vanilla
3 cups QUAKER® Oats (quick
  or old fashioned,
  uncooked)

1 cup all-purpose flour
½ teaspoon baking soda
⅔ cup finely chopped nuts
One 6- to 7-ounce package milk
  chocolate candy stars or
  kisses

Heat oven to 350°F. Lightly grease cookie sheet. Beat margarine and sugar until fluffy. Blend in egg and vanilla. Add combined oats, flour and baking soda; mix well. Shape into 1-inch balls; roll in nuts. Place on prepared cookie sheet. Bake 10 to 12 minutes or until light golden brown. Remove from oven; gently press chocolate candy into center of each cookie. Cool 2 minutes on cookie sheet; remove to wire rack. Cool completely. Store tightly covered.

Makes 3½ dozen cookies

Notes:
Dough may be covered and stored in the refrigerator for up to two days.

Candied cherries may be substituted for chocolate candy, if desired.

From the Cookie Jar

PEANUT BUTTER SPRITZ SANDWICHES

1 package DUNCAN HINES®
  Peanut Butter
  Cookie Mix

1 egg
3 bars (1.55 ounces each)
  milk chocolate

1. Preheat oven to 375°F.

2. Combine cookie mix, contents of peanut butter packet from Mix and egg in large bowl. Stir until thoroughly blended. Fill cookie press with dough. Press desired shapes 2 inches apart onto ungreased baking sheets. Bake at 375°F for 7 to 9 minutes or until set but not browned. Cool 1 minute on baking sheets.

3. Cut each milk chocolate bar into 12 sections by following division marks on bars.

4. To assemble, carefully remove one cookie from baking sheet. Place one milk chocolate section on bottom of warm cookie; top with second cookie. Press together to make sandwich. Repeat with remaining cookies. Place sandwich cookies on cooling racks until chocolate is set. Store in airtight container.   *Makes 2½ to 3 dozen sandwich cookies*

Tip: For best appearance, use cookie press plates that give solid shapes.

Peanut Butter Spritz Sandwiches

Pineapple-Raisin Jumbles

PINEAPPLE-RAISIN JUMBLES

2 cans (8 ounces each)
   DOLE® Crushed
   Pineapple in Juice
$\frac{1}{2}$ cup margarine, softened
$\frac{1}{2}$ cup sugar
1 teaspoon vanilla extract
1 cup all-purpose flour

4 teaspoons grated DOLE®
   Orange peel
1 cup DOLE® Blanched
   Slivered Almonds,
   toasted
1 cup DOLE® Raisins

• Drain pineapple well, pressing out excess liquid with back of spoon. Reserve juice for beverage.

• Beat margarine and sugar in large bowl until light and fluffy. Stir in drained pineapple and vanilla. Beat in flour and orange peel. Stir in almonds and raisins.

• Drop by heaping tablespoonfuls, 2 inches apart, onto greased cookie sheets.

• Bake in 350°F oven 20 to 22 minutes until firm. Cool on wire racks.
Makes 2 to 2½ dozen cookies

CHUNKY BUTTER CHRISTMAS COOKIES

1¼ cups butter, softened
1 cup packed brown sugar
½ cup dairy sour cream
1 egg
2 teaspoons vanilla
1½ cups all-purpose flour
1 teaspoon baking soda
1 teaspoon salt

1½ cups old fashioned or
    quick oats, uncooked
1 package (10 ounces)
    vanilla milk chips
1 cup flaked coconut
1 jar (3½ ounces)
    macadamia nuts,
    coarsely chopped

Beat butter and brown sugar in large bowl until light and fluffy. Blend in sour cream, egg and vanilla. Combine flour, baking soda and salt. Add to butter mixture; mix well. Stir in oats, vanilla milk chips, coconut and nuts. Drop rounded teaspoonfuls of dough, 2 inches apart, onto ungreased cookie sheet.

Bake at 375°F for 10 to 12 minutes or until edges are lightly browned. Cool on cookie sheet 1 minute. Remove to cooling rack; cool completely.

Makes 5 dozen cookies

Favorite recipe from Wisconsin Milk Marketing Board

ORANGE SUGAR COOKIES

2 cups all-purpose flour
1½ teaspoons baking soda
½ cup FLEISCHMANN'S®
    Margarine, softened
1 cup sugar

2 teaspoons grated orange
    peel
1 teaspoon vanilla extract
¼ cup EGG BEATERS® 99%
    Real Egg Product
Additional sugar (optional)

In small bowl, combine flour and baking soda; set aside.

In medium bowl with electric mixer at medium speed, beat margarine, 1 cup sugar, orange peel and vanilla until creamy. Add egg product; beat until smooth. Gradually stir in flour mixture until blended. Cover; chill dough 1 hour.

Shape dough into 42 (¾-inch) balls; roll in additional sugar if desired. Place on lightly greased baking sheets, about 2 inches apart. Bake at 375°F for 8 to 10 minutes or until light golden brown. Remove from sheets; cool on wire racks.

Makes 3½ dozen cookies

PINEAPPLE-OATMEAL COOKIES

1 can (20 ounces) DOLE®
    Crushed Pineapple in
    Syrup*
1¹/₂ cups brown sugar, packed
1 cup margarine
1 egg
3 cups rolled oats, uncooked
2 cups all-purpose flour

1 teaspoon baking powder
1 teaspoon ground
    cinnamon
¹/₂ teaspoon salt
1 cup DOLE® Raisins
1 cup DOLE® Natural
    Almonds, toasted and
    chopped

• Drain pineapple well. Reserve ¹/₂ cup syrup.

• Beat sugar and margarine in large bowl until light and fluffy. Beat in egg, drained pineapple and reserved ¹/₂ cup syrup. Combine remaining ingredients in medium bowl; blend into pineapple mixture.

• Drop by 2 heaping tablespoonfuls, 2 inches apart, onto greased cookie sheets. Flatten tops with back of spoon.

• Bake in 350°F oven 20 to 25 minutes until golden. Cool on wire racks.

Makes about 2¹/₂ dozen cookies

*Use pineapple packed in juice, if desired.

AUNTIE VAN'S CHRISTMAS COOKIES

2 cups granulated sugar
1 cup butter, softened
2 eggs
1 teaspoon vanilla
5 cups all-purpose flour

1 teaspoon baking soda
1 cup sour cream
    Coffee Frosting (page 45)
    or canned vanilla
    frosting

Beat granulated sugar and 1 cup butter in large bowl until light and fluffy. Blend in eggs and 1 teaspoon vanilla. Combine flour and baking soda; add alternately with sour cream, mixing well after each addition. Refrigerate 6 hours or overnight. Divide dough into 4 pieces. Roll out 1 piece on lightly floured surface to ¹/₈-inch thickness (keep remaining dough refrigerated). Cut into desired shapes; place on ungreased cookie sheets. Bake at 325°F for 10 to 12 minutes or until bottoms are golden brown. Repeat with remaining dough. Cool completely. Frost with Coffee Frosting.

Makes 6 dozen cookies
Continued

COFFEE FROSTING

1 tablespoon instant coffee
   granules
1 tablespoon hot water
6 tablespoons butter,
   softened

1 teaspoon vanilla
3 cups sifted powdered sugar
¼ to ⅓ cup whipping cream

Dissolve coffee granules in water. Beat 6 tablespoons butter in medium bowl until soft. Stir in coffee mixture and 1 teaspoon vanilla. Add powdered sugar; mix until well combined. Gradually add cream until good spreading consistency.

Favorite recipe from Wisconsin Milk Marketing Board

SESAME-ALMOND COOKIES

1 cup FILIPPO BERIO® Brand
   Olive Oil
1 (2-inch) strip lemon peel
4 teaspoons sesame seeds
½ cup dry white wine
1 teaspoon grated lemon
   peel

1 teaspoon grated orange
   peel
⅓ cup sugar
½ cup sliced almonds
3½ cups all-purpose flour
1 tablespoon ground
   cinnamon

1. Heat oil, 2-inch strip lemon peel and sesame seeds in large skillet over medium heat until seeds are lightly browned. Remove from heat; cool.

2. Remove lemon peel strip. Pour oil and sesame seeds into large bowl. Add wine, grated lemon and orange peels, sugar and almonds; stir.

3. Combine flour and cinnamon in small bowl. Add to oil mixture gradually, stirring well. Gather dough into ball; knead once or twice until smooth. Set aside to rest for 30 minutes.

4. Preheat oven to 350°F. Divide dough into 18 equal pieces. Roll each into a ball and flatten to about 3 inches across and ¼ inch thick. Place on lightly greased baking sheet. Bake 20 minutes or until lightly browned and firm. Cool on wire rack. Store in covered container.

Makes 18 cookies

MARVELOUS MACAROONS

1 can (8 ounces) DOLE®
    Crushed Pineapple in
    Juice
1 can (14 ounces) sweetened
    condensed milk
1 package (7 ounces) flaked
    coconut

½ cup DOLE® Chopped
    Almonds, toasted
½ cup margarine, melted
    Grated peel from 1 DOLE®
    Lemon
¼ teaspoon almond extract
1 cup all-purpose flour
1 teaspoon baking powder

• Drain pineapple well. Reserve juice for beverage.

• Combine drained pineapple, sweetened condensed milk, coconut, almonds, margarine, 1 teaspoon lemon peel and almond extract in large bowl; mix well.

• Combine flour and baking powder in small bowl. Beat into pineapple mixture until blended.

• Drop by heaping tablespoonfuls, 1 inch apart, onto greased cookie sheets.

• Bake in 350°F oven 13 to 15 minutes. Cool on wire racks. Store in refrigerator.   *Makes 3½ dozen cookies*

FAVORITE PEANUT BUTTER COOKIES

½ cup peanut butter
¼ cup (½ stick) margarine or
    butter, softened
¾ cup sugar
1 egg, beaten

½ cup all-purpose flour
½ teaspoon baking powder
¼ teaspoon salt (optional)
2 cups Rice CHEX® brand
    cereal, crushed to 1 cup

Preheat oven to 350°F. Lightly grease cookie sheet. In large bowl, cream peanut butter, margarine and sugar. Add egg. Stir in flour and baking powder; add salt, if desired. Stir in cereal; mix well. For each cookie, roll 1 level tablespoon dough into ball. Place on prepared cookie sheet. With fork dipped in sugar, flatten slightly in criss-cross pattern. Bake 8 to 10 minutes or until bottoms are lightly browned. Let stand 1 minute before removing from cookie sheet. Cool on wire rack.

Makes 2½ dozen cookies

Marvelous Macaroons

MERRY SUGAR COOKIES

2¼ cups all-purpose flour
1 teaspoon baking soda
½ teaspoon baking powder
¼ teaspoon salt
1 cup (2 sticks) butter or
   margarine, softened
1½ cups sugar

1 egg
1 teaspoon vanilla extract
One 9-ounce package
   (1½ cups) NESTLÉ® Toll
   House® semi-sweet
   chocolate Merry
   Morsels®, divided

Preheat oven to 375°F. In small bowl, combine flour, baking soda, baking powder and salt; set aside.

In large mixer bowl, beat butter and sugar until creamy. Blend in egg and vanilla extract. Gradually beat in flour mixture. (Batter will be stiff.) Stir in 1 cup Nestlé Toll House semi-sweet chocolate Merry Morsels. Shape rounded teaspoonfuls dough into balls; place on ungreased cookie sheets. Gently press 3 or 4 remaining Merry Morsels into each ball.

Bake 8 to 10 minutes until edges are lightly browned. Let stand 2 minutes. Remove from cookie sheets; cool.

Makes about 4½ dozen cookies

SNICKERDOODLES

1 cup BUTTER FLAVOR
   CRISCO®
1¾ cups sugar, divided
2 eggs
1 teaspoon vanilla

2¼ cups all-purpose flour
2 teaspoons cream of tartar
1 teaspoon baking soda
¾ teaspoon salt
1 teaspoon cinnamon

1. Preheat oven to 400°F.

2. Cream Butter Flavor Crisco, 1½ cups sugar, eggs and vanilla thoroughly in large bowl at medium speed of electric mixer. Combine flour, cream of tartar, baking soda and salt. Stir into creamed mixture.

3. Shape into 1-inch balls. Combine remaining ¼ cup sugar and cinnamon in small bowl. Roll balls of dough in cinnamon-sugar mixture. Place 2 inches apart on ungreased baking sheets.

4. Bake at 400°F for 7 to 8 minutes. Remove to wire racks to cool completely.

Makes 6 dozen cookies

Merry Sugar Cookies

PEANUT BUTTER PIZZA COOKIES

2 packages DUNCAN HINES®
    Peanut Butter
    Cookie Mix
2 eggs
1 tablespoon water
    Sugar
1 container (16 ounces)
    DUNCAN HINES®
    Chocolate Layer Cake
    Frosting

Cashews
Candy-coated chocolate
    pieces
Gumdrops, halved
Flaked coconut
1 bar (2 ounces) white
    chocolate baking bar
1 tablespoon CRISCO®
    Shortening

1. Preheat oven to 375°F.

2. For cookies, place cookie mixes in large bowl. Break up any lumps. Add eggs, contents of peanut butter packets from Mixes and water. Stir until thoroughly blended. Shape into 18 (2-inch) balls (about 3 level tablespoons each). Place 3½ inches apart on ungreased baking sheets. Flatten with bottom of large glass dipped in sugar to make 3-inch circles. Bake at 375°F for 9 to 11 minutes or until set. Cool 1 minute on baking sheets. Remove to cooling racks. Cool completely.

3. Frost cookies with Chocolate frosting. Decorate with cashews, chocolate pieces, gumdrops and coconut. Melt white chocolate and shortening in small saucepan on low heat, stirring constantly until smooth. Drizzle over cookies. *Makes 18 (3-inch) cookies*

CAP'N'S COOKIES

1 cup firmly packed brown
    sugar
½ cup (1 stick) margarine or
    butter, softened
2 eggs
1 teaspoon vanilla
1½ cups all-purpose flour

1 teaspoon baking powder
½ teaspoon salt (optional)
2 cups CAP'N CRUNCH®
    Cereal, any flavor,
    coarsely crushed
1 cup raisins or semi-sweet
    chocolate pieces

Heat oven to 375°F. Lightly grease cookie sheet. Beat sugar and margarine until fluffy. Blend in eggs and vanilla. Add combined flour, baking powder and salt; mix well. Stir in cereal and raisins. Drop by rounded teaspoonfuls onto prepared cookie sheet. Bake 10 to 12 minutes or until light golden brown. Cool 2 minutes on cookie sheet; remove to wire rack. Cool completely. Store tightly covered. *Makes about 3 dozen cookies*

Peanut Butter Pizza Cookies

Mini Morsel Granola Cookies and Banana Bars (page 63)

MINI MORSEL GRANOLA COOKIES

2½ cups all-purpose flour
2 teaspoons baking powder
1 teaspoon baking soda
1 teaspoon cinnamon
1 cup (2 sticks) butter, softened
1¼ cups firmly packed brown sugar

2 eggs
One 12-ounce package (2 cups) NESTLE® Toll House® semi-sweet chocolate mini morsels
2 cups granola cereal
1 cup raisins

Preheat oven to 375°F. In small bowl, combine flour, baking powder, baking soda and cinnamon; set aside.

In large mixer bowl, beat butter and brown sugar until creamy. Beat in eggs. Gradually beat in flour mixture. Stir in Nestlé Toll House semi-sweet chocolate mini morsels, granola and raisins. Drop by rounded measuring tablespoonfuls onto ungreased cookie sheets.

Bake 9 to 11 minutes until edges are golden brown. Let stand on cookie sheets 5 minutes. Remove from cookie sheets; cool.

Makes about 4 dozen cookies

NORWEGIAN MOLASSES COOKIES

2¼ cups all-purpose flour
2 teaspoons baking soda
1 cup firmly packed light
    brown sugar
¾ cup FLEISCHMANN'S®
    Margarine, softened
¼ cup EGG BEATERS® 99%
    Real Egg Product

¼ cup BRER RABBIT® Light
    or Dark Molasses
¼ cup granulated sugar
Water
Confectioner's Sugar Glaze
    (recipe follows) (optional)
Colored sprinkles
    (optional)

In small bowl, combine flour and baking soda; set aside.

In medium bowl with electric mixer at medium speed, cream brown sugar and margarine. Add egg product and molasses; beat until smooth. Stir in flour mixture. Cover; chill dough 1 hour.

Shape dough into 48 (1¼-inch) balls; roll in granulated sugar. Place on greased and floured baking sheets, about 2 inches apart. Lightly sprinkle dough with water. Bake at 350°F for 18 to 20 minutes or until flattened. Remove from sheets; cool on wire racks. Decorate with Confectioner's Sugar Glaze and colored sprinkles if desired.   *Makes 4 dozen cookies*

Confectioner's Sugar Glaze: Combine 1 cup confectioner's sugar and 5 to 6 teaspoons skim milk.

GIANT OATMEAL COOKIES

1 cup firmly packed brown
    sugar
¾ cup (1½ sticks) margarine
    or butter, softened
2 eggs
1 teaspoon vanilla
1¼ cups all-purpose flour
½ teaspoon baking soda

½ teaspoon salt (optional)
2½ cups QUAKER® Oats (quick
    or old fashioned,
    uncooked)
One 6-ounce package (1 cup)
    semi-sweet chocolate
    pieces
½ cup chopped nuts

Heat oven to 350°F. Lightly grease 2 large cookie sheets. Beat sugar and margarine until fluffy. Blend in eggs and vanilla. Add combined flour, baking soda, salt and oats; mix well. Stir in chocolate pieces and nuts. Divide dough in half. Press each half into circle about ¾ inch thick on prepared cookie sheets. Bake 17 to 20 minutes or until lightly browned. Cool 5 minutes on cookie sheets; remove to wire racks. Cool completely. Cut into wedges to serve.   *Makes 2 giant cookies*

Variation: Drop dough by rounded tablespoonfuls onto greased cookie sheets. Bake 10 to 12 minutes. Makes about 3 dozen cookies.

OATMEAL SCOTCHIES

1¼ cups all-purpose flour
1 teaspoon baking soda
½ teaspoon salt
½ teaspoon cinnamon
1 cup (2 sticks) butter, softened
¾ cup granulated sugar
¾ cup firmly packed brown sugar
2 eggs

1 teaspoon vanilla extract *or* grated peel of 1 orange
3 cups quick or old fashioned oats, uncooked
One 12-ounce package (2 cups) NESTLÉ® Toll House® butterscotch flavored morsels

Preheat oven to 375°F. In small bowl, combine flour, baking soda, salt and cinnamon; set aside.

In large mixer bowl, beat butter, granulated sugar, brown sugar, eggs and vanilla extract until creamy. Gradually beat in flour mixture. Stir in oats and Nestlé Toll House butterscotch flavored morsels. Drop by measuring tablespoonfuls onto ungreased cookie sheets. Bake 7 to 8 minutes for chewier cookies (9 to 10 minutes for crisper cookies). Remove from cookie sheets; cool completely.   *Makes about 4 dozen cookies*

PEANUT BUTTER COOKIES

⅔ cup firmly packed light brown sugar
½ cup chunky or smooth peanut butter
⅓ cup BLUE BONNET® Margarine, softened
1 egg

½ cup Regular, Instant or Quick CREAM OF WHEAT® Cereal
1 teaspoon vanilla extract
1¼ cups all-purpose flour
½ teaspoon baking soda

In medium bowl with electric mixer at medium speed, beat brown sugar, peanut butter, margarine and egg until fluffy; blend in cereal and vanilla. Stir in flour and baking soda to make a stiff dough.

Shape dough into 1-inch balls. Place 2 inches apart on greased baking sheets. Flatten balls with bottom of floured glass; press with fork tines to make criss-cross pattern. Bake at 350°F for 8 to 9 minutes or until lightly browned. Remove from sheets; cool on wire racks.
Makes 4 dozen cookies

Oatmeal Scotchies

Lunch Box Lollipops

FAMOUS OATMEAL COOKIES

¾ cup vegetable shortening
1 cup firmly packed brown
  sugar
½ cup granulated sugar
1 egg
¼ cup water
1 teaspoon vanilla

3 cups QUAKER® Oats (quick
  or old fashioned,
  uncooked)
1 cup all-purpose flour
1 teaspoon salt (optional)
½ teaspoon baking soda

Heat oven to 350°F. Beat shortening, sugars, egg, water and vanilla until creamy. Add combined oats, flour, salt and baking soda; mix well. Drop by rounded teaspoonfuls onto ungreased cookie sheet. Bake 12 to 15 minutes or until light golden brown. Remove to cooling rack; cool completely. Store tightly covered. *Makes about 5 dozen cookies*

My Own Special Cookies: Add 1 cup of any or a combination of the following ingredients to basic cookie dough: raisins, chopped nuts, chocolate chips or coconut. Makes about 5 dozen cookies.

LUNCH BOX LOLLIPOPS

2 extra-ripe, medium DOLE®
   Bananas
¾ cup brown sugar, packed
¾ cup margarine, softened
1 egg
1¾ cups quick-cooking oats
1½ cups all-purpose flour
1 teaspoon ground
   cinnamon

½ teaspoon ground nutmeg
½ teaspoon baking soda
½ teaspoon salt
1½ cups DOLE® Raisins
1 cup DOLE® Chopped
   Almonds
4 dozen wooden popsicle
   sticks (optional)

• Place bananas in blender. Process until puréed; use 1 cup for recipe.

• Beat brown sugar and margarine in large bowl until light and fluffy. Beat in egg, then 1 cup banana.

• Combine oats, flour, cinnamon, nutmeg, baking soda and salt in small bowl; stir into banana mixture just until blended. Stir in raisins and almonds.

• Drop by 2 heaping tablespoonfuls, 2 inches apart, onto lightly greased cookie sheets. Push popsicle stick into center of each, if desired. Flatten tops of cookies with back of spoon.

• Bake in 350°F oven 15 to 18 minutes until lightly browned. Cool on wire racks. *Makes 3½ to 4 dozen cookies*

SOFT RAISIN COOKIES

1 cup butter, softened
¾ cup packed brown sugar
½ cup granulated sugar
2 eggs
1½ teaspoons vanilla
3 cups all-purpose flour
½ cup wheat germ

2 teaspoons baking powder
¾ teaspoon baking soda
½ teaspoon salt
½ teaspoon nutmeg
½ cup milk
1 cup raisins

Beat butter, sugars, eggs and vanilla in large mixer bowl. Combine flour, wheat germ, baking powder, baking soda, salt and nutmeg in medium bowl. Add to butter mixture alternately with milk, mixing well after each addition. Stir in raisins. Drop dough by teaspoonfuls, 2 inches apart, onto ungreased cookie sheets. Bake in 350°F oven 10 to 12 minutes or until light brown. Immediately remove to wire racks to cool.

Makes about 7 dozen cookies

Favorite recipe from Wisconsin Milk Marketing Board

Outrageous Brownies & Bars

Rich brownies and delicious bar cookies are quick to make and will satisfy the cookie monster in your house.

ONE BOWL BROWNIES

4 squares BAKER'S®
    Unsweetened Chocolate
¾ cup (1½ sticks) margarine
    or butter
2 cups sugar

3 eggs
1 teaspoon vanilla
1 cup all-purpose flour
1 cup chopped nuts
    (optional)

Heat oven to 350°F. Microwave chocolate and margarine in large microwavable bowl on HIGH 2 minutes or until margarine is melted. Stir until chocolate is completely melted. Stir sugar into melted chocolate mixture. Mix in eggs and vanilla until well blended. Stir in flour and nuts. Spread in greased 13×9-inch pan.

Bake 30 to 35 minutes or until toothpick inserted into center comes out with fudgy crumbs. *Do not overbake.* Cool in pan; cut into bars.

Makes about 24 brownies

Prep time: 10 minutes
Baking time: 30 to 35 minutes

Tips:
• For cakelike brownies, stir in ½ cup milk with eggs and vanilla. Increase flour to 1½ cups.

• When using a glass baking dish, reduce oven temperature to 325°F.

Continued on page 60

Top to bottom: Peanut Butter Swirl Brownies (page 60); Rocky Road Brownies (page 60)

Rocky Road Brownies: Prepare One Bowl Brownies as directed. Bake at 350°F for 30 minutes. Sprinkle 2 cups KRAFT® Miniature Marshmallows, 1 cup BAKER'S® Semi-Sweet Real Chocolate Chips and 1 cup chopped nuts over brownies immediately. Continue baking 3 to 5 minutes or until topping begins to melt together. Cool in pan; cut into bars. Makes about 24 brownies.

Prep time: 15 minutes
Baking time: 35 minutes

Peanut Butter Swirl Brownies: Prepare One Bowl Brownie batter as directed, reserving 1 tablespoon margarine and 2 tablespoons sugar. Spread batter in greased 13×9-inch pan. Add reserved ingredients to 2/3 cup peanut butter; mix well. Place spoonfuls of peanut butter mixture over brownie batter. Swirl with knife to marbleize. Bake at 350°F for 30 to 35 minutes or until toothpick inserted into center comes out with fudgy crumbs. Cool in pan; cut into bars. Makes about 24 brownies.

Prep time: 15 minutes
Baking time: 30 to 35 minutes

PECAN TURTLE BARS

1½ cups all-purpose flour
1½ cups packed brown sugar, divided
½ cup butter, softened

1 cup pecan halves
2/3 cup butter
1 cup milk chocolate pieces

Combine flour, 1 cup brown sugar and softened butter in large mixer bowl. Beat at medium speed of electric mixer 2 to 3 minutes or until mixture resembles fine crumbs. Pat mixture evenly onto bottom of ungreased 13×9-inch baking pan. Sprinkle pecans evenly over crumb mixture.

Combine 2/3 cup butter and remaining ½ cup brown sugar in small saucepan. Cook and stir over medium heat until entire surface is bubbly. Cook and stir ½ to 1 minute more. Pour into pan, spreading evenly over crust. Bake in 350°F oven 18 to 20 minutes or until entire surface is bubbly. Remove from oven; immediately sprinkle with chocolate pieces. Let stand 2 to 3 minutes to allow chocolate to melt; use knife to swirl chocolate slightly. Cool completely in pan on wire rack. Use sharp knife to cut into 48 bars. *Makes 48 bars*

Favorite recipe from Wisconsin Milk Marketing Board

BLACK RUSSIAN BROWNIES

4 squares (1 ounce *each*)
   unsweetened chocolate
1 cup butter
3/4 teaspoon black pepper
4 eggs, lightly beaten
1 1/2 cups sugar
1 1/2 teaspoons vanilla
1/3 cup KAHLÚA®

2 tablespoons vodka
1 1/3 cups all-purpose flour
1/2 teaspoon salt
1/4 teaspoon baking powder
1 cup chopped walnuts or
   toasted sliced almonds
Powdered sugar (optional)

Line bottom of 13×9-inch baking pan with waxed paper. Melt chocolate and butter with pepper in small saucepan over low heat. Remove from heat.

Combine eggs, sugar and vanilla in large bowl; beat well. Stir in cooled chocolate mixture, Kahlúa and vodka. Combine flour, salt and baking powder; add to chocolate mixture and stir until blended. Add walnuts. Spread in prepared pan.

Bake in 350°F oven just until toothpick inserted into center comes out clean, about 25 minutes. *Do not overbake.* Cool in pan on wire rack. Cut into bars. Sprinkle with powdered sugar, if desired.

Makes about 30 brownies

BAKED S'MORES

1 package DUNCAN HINES®
   Golden Sugar Cookie Mix
1 egg
1 tablespoon water

3 bars (1.55 ounces each)
   milk chocolate
1 jar (7 ounces)
   marshmallow creme

1. Preheat oven to 350°F. Grease 8-inch square pan.

2. Combine cookie mix, contents of buttery flavor packet from Mix, egg and water in large bowl. Stir until thoroughly blended. Divide cookie dough in half. Press half the dough evenly into bottom of pan.

3. Cut each milk chocolate bar into 12 sections by following division marks on bars. Arrange chocolate sections into 4 rows, with 9 sections in each row.

4. Place spoonfuls of marshmallow creme on top of chocolate. Spread to cover chocolate and cookie dough. Drop remaining cookie dough by teaspoonfuls on top of marshmallow creme. Spread slightly with back of spoon. Bake at 350°F for 25 to 30 minutes or until light golden brown. Cool completely. Cut into squares.

Makes 9 squares

FRUIT AND CHOCOLATE DREAM SQUARES

TOPPING
- ²/₃ cup all-purpose flour
- ¹/₂ cup pecans, chopped
- ¹/₃ cup firmly packed brown sugar
- 6 tablespoons (³/₄ stick) butter, softened

CRUST
- 1¹/₄ cups all-purpose flour
- ¹/₂ cup granulated sugar
- ¹/₂ cup (1 stick) butter
- ¹/₂ cup strawberry or raspberry jam
- One 10-ounce package (1¹/₂ cups) NESTLÉ® Toll House® Treasures® milk chocolate deluxe baking pieces

Topping: In small bowl, combine ²/₃ cup flour, pecans and brown sugar. With pastry blender or 2 knives, cut in 6 tablespoons butter until mixture resembles coarse crumbs; set aside.

Crust: Preheat oven to 375°F. Grease 9-inch square baking pan. In small bowl, combine 1¹/₄ cups flour and granulated sugar. With pastry blender or 2 knives, cut in ¹/₂ cup butter until mixture resembles fine crumbs. Press into prepared pan.

Bake 20 to 25 minutes until set but not brown. Spread with jam. Top with Nestlé Toll House Treasures milk chocolate deluxe baking pieces and Topping.

Bake 15 to 20 minutes longer until top is lightly browned. Cool completely; cut into 2¹/₄-inch squares. *Makes 16 squares*

PEANUT BUTTER-RAISIN BARS

- ¹/₄ cup firmly packed light brown sugar
- ¹/₄ cup corn syrup
- ¹/₄ cup chunky peanut butter
- 2 cups SPOON SIZE® Shredded Wheat, coarsely crushed
- ³/₄ cup seedless raisins

In large saucepan over medium heat, stir together brown sugar and corn syrup until sugar dissolves and mixture is warm. Remove from heat; blend in peanut butter. Stir in cereal and raisins until well coated. Press into lightly greased 8×8-inch baking pan. Cool until firm. Cut into 24 bars. Store in airtight container. *Makes 24 bars*

Fruit and Chocolate Dream Squares

BANANA BARS

1½ cups all-purpose flour
½ cup whole wheat flour
2 teaspoons baking powder
½ teaspoon salt
¾ cup (1½ sticks) butter, softened
⅔ cup granulated sugar
⅔ cup firmly packed light brown sugar

1 teaspoon vanilla extract
2 medium bananas, mashed
1 egg
One 12-ounce package (2 cups) NESTLE® Toll House® semi-sweet chocolate mini morsels
Confectioners' sugar

Preheat oven to 350°F. In small bowl, combine flours, baking powder and salt; set aside.

In large mixer bowl, beat butter, granulated sugar, brown sugar and vanilla extract until creamy. Beat in bananas and egg. Gradually beat in flour mixture. Stir in Nestlé Toll House semi-sweet chocolate mini morsels. Spread into greased 15½ × 10½-inch baking pan.

Bake 25 to 30 minutes. Cool completely. Sprinkle with confectioners' sugar. Cut into 2 × 1-inch bars.   *Makes about 6½ dozen bars*

Variation: Omit whole wheat flour. Increase all-purpose flour to 2 cups.

PINEAPPLE PECAN BARS

CRUST
2 cups all-purpose flour
²/₃ cup powdered sugar

1 cup margarine

PINEAPPLE TOPPING
1 can (20 ounces) DOLE®
Crushed Pineapple in
Syrup or Juice, drained
4 eggs

¾ cup brown sugar, packed
⅓ cup all-purpose flour
2 cups coarsely chopped
pecans

For crust, combine 2 cups flour and powdered sugar. Cut in margarine until mixture is crumbly. Press into bottom of 13×9-inch baking pan. Bake in 350°F oven 15 minutes. Remove from oven.

For topping, combine drained pineapple, eggs, brown sugar and ⅓ cup flour. Stir in pecans. Pour over partially baked crust. Bake in 350°F oven 30 to 35 minutes or until set. Cool completely. Cut into bars.

Makes 32 bars

MALLOW-GRAHAM BARS

2 tablespoons BLUE
BONNET® Margarine
3 cups marshmallows
1 stay fresh package HONEY
MAID® Honey Grahams,
coarsely chopped

½ cup seedless raisins
½ cup chopped dry roasted
peanuts

In large saucepan over low heat, melt margarine. Add marshmallows; stir until melted. Remove from heat; stir in graham crackers, raisins and peanuts. Spread mixture into greased 9×9-inch baking pan. Cool 1 hour or until firm. Cut into 18 bars. Store in airtight container.

Makes 18 bars

Pineapple Pecan Bars

CHOCOLATE PECAN PIE BARS

CRUST
1½ cups all-purpose flour
½ cup (1 stick) butter,
 softened

¼ cup firmly packed brown
 sugar

FILLING
3 eggs
¾ cup dark or light corn
 syrup
¾ cup granulated sugar
2 tablespoons (¼ stick)
 butter, melted
1 teaspoon vanilla extract

1½ cups coarsely chopped
 pecans
One 10-ounce package
 (1½ cups) NESTLÉ® Toll
 House® Treasures® semi-
 sweet chocolate deluxe
 baking pieces

Crust: Preheat oven to 350°F. In small mixer bowl, beat flour, ½ cup butter and brown sugar until crumbly. Press into greased 13×9-inch baking pan. Bake 12 to 15 minutes until lightly browned.

Filling: In medium bowl with wire whisk, beat eggs, corn syrup, granulated sugar, melted butter and vanilla extract. Stir in pecans and Nestlé Toll House Treasures semi-sweet chocolate deluxe baking pieces. Pour evenly over baked crust.

Bake 25 to 30 minutes until set. Cool; cut into 2×1½-inch bars.
Makes about 3 dozen bars

FUDGY CHEESECAKE SWIRL BROWNIES

CREAM CHEESE BATTER
One 8-ounce package cream
 cheese, softened
½ cup sugar

1 egg
1 teaspoon vanilla extract

CHOCOLATE BATTER
¾ cup (1½ sticks) butter
2 foil-wrapped bars
 (4 ounces) NESTLÉ®
 unsweetened chocolate
 baking bars

1¾ cups sugar
3 eggs, well beaten
1¾ cups all-purpose flour

Continued

Fudgy Cheesecake Swirl Brownies

Cream Cheese Batter: Preheat oven to 350°F. In small mixer bowl, beat cream cheese and ½ cup sugar until smooth. Beat in 1 egg and vanilla extract; set aside.

Chocolate Batter: In heavy-gauge, medium saucepan over low heat, melt butter and Nestlé unsweetened chocolate baking bars, stirring until smooth. Stir in 1¾ cups sugar. Blend in 3 eggs. Stir in flour.

Spread Chocolate Batter into greased 13×9-inch baking pan. Spoon Cream Cheese Batter over top. Swirl metal spatula through batters to marbleize.

Bake 30 to 35 minutes until edges begin to pull away from sides of pan. Cool completely; cut into 2-inch bars.

Makes about 2 dozen brownies

Chocolate Apple Crisp

CHOCOLATE APPLE CRISP

1½ cups all-purpose flour
1 cup firmly packed brown
   sugar
½ teaspoon baking soda
¼ teaspoon salt
¾ cup (1½ sticks) butter
1½ cups quick oats, uncooked

One 12-ounce package (2 cups)
   NESTLÉ® Toll House®
   semi-sweet chocolate
   mini morsels, divided
3 apples, unpeeled if
   desired, chopped
1 cup pecans or walnuts,
   chopped

Preheat oven to 375°F. In large bowl, combine flour, brown sugar, baking soda and salt. With pastry blender or 2 knives, cut in butter until mixture resembles fine crumbs. Stir in oats; press half of oat mixture into greased 13×9-inch baking pan.

To remaining oat mixture, add Nestlé Toll House semi-sweet chocolate mini morsels, apples and pecans; stir to combine. Sprinkle over base.

Bake 35 to 40 minutes until lightly browned. Cool slightly; cut into squares. *Makes about 15 servings*

MOCHA BROWNIES

1¼ cups all-purpose flour
1 teaspoon baking powder
½ teaspoon salt
4 (1-ounce) squares
   semisweet chocolate
¾ cup BLUE BONNET®
   Margarine
1 tablespoon instant coffee
   granules

1 cup granulated sugar
4 eggs
1 teaspoon vanilla extract
1¼ cups PLANTERS® Walnuts,
   chopped and divided
   Creamy Coffee Frosting
   (recipe follows)

In small bowl, combine flour, baking powder and salt; set aside.

In large saucepan over low heat, stir together chocolate, margarine and
1 tablespoon coffee granules until blended. Remove from heat; stir in
granulated sugar. Add eggs, 1 at a time, beating well after each addition.
Stir in flour mixture and vanilla until blended. Stir in 1 cup walnuts.
Spread in greased 13×9-inch baking pan.

Bake at 350°F for 25 to 30 minutes. Cool in pan on wire rack. Spread
with Creamy Coffee Frosting; sprinkle with remaining ¼ cup walnuts.
Cut into 2×1½-inch bars.   *Makes about 32 bars*

Creamy Coffee Frosting: Dissolve 1 teaspoon instant coffee granules in
¼ cup milk. In small bowl with electric mixer at high speed, beat 4
ounces cream cheese and milk mixture until creamy. Gradually beat in 1
(16-ounce) package confectioner's sugar until well blended and good
spreading consistency.

FROSTED TOFFEE BARS

2 cups QUAKER® Oats (quick
   or old fashioned,
   uncooked)
½ cup firmly packed brown
   sugar

½ cup (1 stick) margarine or
   butter, melted
½ cup semi-sweet chocolate
   pieces
¼ cup chopped peanuts

Heat oven to 350°F. Lightly grease 9-inch square baking pan. In large
bowl, combine oats, brown sugar and margarine; mix well. Spread into
prepared pan. Bake 13 minutes or until light golden brown; cool on wire
rack.

In small saucepan over low heat, melt chocolate pieces. Spread over baked
oat mixture; sprinkle with peanuts. Chill 4 hours or until chocolate is set.
Cut into 2×1½-inch bars. Store tightly covered in refrigerator.
                                             Makes about 28 bars

RICH 'N' CREAMY BROWNIE BARS

BROWNIES

1 package DUNCAN HINES®
   Chocolate Lovers' Double
   Fudge Brownie Mix
2 eggs

⅓ cup water
¼ cup CRISCO® Oil or
   CRISCO® PURITAN® Oil
½ cup chopped pecans

TOPPING

1 package (8 ounces) cream
   cheese, softened
2 eggs

1 pound (3½ cups)
   confectioners sugar
1 teaspoon vanilla extract

1. Preheat oven to 350°F. Grease bottom of 13×9-inch pan.

2. **For brownies,** combine brownie mix, contents of fudge packet from Mix, 2 eggs, water and oil in large bowl. Stir with spoon until well blended, about 50 strokes. Stir in pecans. Spread evenly in pan.

3. **For topping,** beat cream cheese in large bowl at medium speed with electric mixer until smooth. Beat in 2 eggs, confectioners sugar and vanilla extract until smooth. Spread evenly over brownie mixture. Bake at 350°F for 45 to 50 minutes or until edges and top are golden brown and shiny. Cool completely. Refrigerate until well chilled. Cut into bars.

Makes 48 bars

SPICED MINCEMEAT SQUARES

½ cup all-purpose flour
½ teaspoon ground
   cinnamon
¼ teaspoon ground nutmeg
¼ teaspoon baking soda
⅓ cup BLUE BONNET®
   Margarine, softened

½ cup firmly packed light
   brown sugar
1 egg
1 cup prepared mincemeat
1 cup NABISCO® 100% Bran
   Confectioner's Sugar Glaze
   (page 53)

In small bowl, combine flour, cinnamon, nutmeg and baking soda; set aside.

In medium bowl with electric mixer at medium speed, beat margarine and brown sugar until creamy. Beat in egg. Add flour mixture, mincemeat and bran. Spread into greased 9×9-inch baking pan. Bake at 400°F for 20 to 25 minutes or until knife inserted into center comes out clean. Cool on wire rack. Drizzle with Confectioner's Sugar Glaze. Cut into 2¼-inch squares. Store in airtight container.

Makes 16 squares

Rich 'n' Creamy Brownie Bars

YUMMY PEANUT BUTTER BARS

BARS
1 package DUNCAN HINES®
  Peanut Butter
  Cookie Mix

1 egg
1 tablespoon water
1/3 cup chopped peanuts

WHITE GLAZE
1/2 cup confectioners sugar

1 to 2 teaspoons water

CHOCOLATE GLAZE
1/4 cup semi-sweet chocolate
  chips

2 teaspoons CRISCO®
  Shortening

1. Preheat oven to 350°F.

2. **For bars,** combine cookie mix, contents of peanut butter packet from Mix, egg and 1 tablespoon water in large bowl. Stir until thoroughly blended. Stir in peanuts. Spread in ungreased 8-inch square pan. Bake at 350°F for 23 to 25 minutes or until edges are light golden brown. Cool completely.

3. **For white glaze,** place confectioners sugar in small bowl. Add water, 1 teaspoon at a time, stirring until smooth and desired consistency. Drizzle over cooled bars.

4. **For chocolate glaze,** place chocolate chips and shortening in small resealable plastic bag; seal. Place bag in bowl of hot water for several minutes. Dry with paper towel. Knead until blended and chocolate is smooth. Snip pinpoint hole in corner of bag. Drizzle chocolate glaze over white glaze. Allow glazes to set before cutting into bars.

Makes 18 bars

Tip: For a special presentation, cut cookies into diamond or triangle shapes instead of bars.

RASPBERRY MERINGUE BARS

1 cup butter or margarine,
  softened
1/2 cup firmly packed brown
  sugar

1 egg
2 cups all-purpose flour
1 can SOLO® *or* 1 jar BAKER®
  Raspberry Filling

MERINGUE TOPPING
3 egg whites
3/4 cup granulated sugar

1/2 cup shredded coconut
1/2 cup slivered almonds

Continued

Preheat oven to 325°F. Grease 13×9-inch baking pan. Beat butter and brown sugar in medium bowl with electric mixer at medium speed until light and fluffy. Add 1 egg; beat until blended. Stir in flour until well combined. Pat dough evenly in prepared pan. Bake 20 minutes. Remove from oven; spread raspberry filling over crust. (Do not turn oven off.)

For meringue topping, beat egg whites in medium bowl with electric mixer at high speed until soft peaks form. Add granulated sugar gradually; beat until stiff and glossy. Fold coconut and almonds into beaten egg white mixture. Spread over raspberry filling. Return to oven. Bake 20 minutes or until meringue topping is lightly browned. Cool completely in pan on wire rack. Cut into 48 bars.   *Makes 48 bars*

KAHLÚA® MUDSLIDE BROWNIES

2 cups all-purpose flour
$\frac{1}{2}$ teaspoon baking powder
$\frac{1}{2}$ teaspoon salt
$\frac{2}{3}$ cup butter
4 squares (1 ounce *each*) unsweetened chocolate, chopped
3 eggs
$1\frac{1}{2}$ cups granulated sugar
4 tablespoons KAHLÚA®
2 tablespoons Irish cream liqueur
1 tablespoon vodka
$\frac{3}{4}$ cup coarsely chopped walnuts (optional)
Kahlúa® Glaze (recipe follows)
Whole coffee beans (optional)

Combine flour, baking powder and salt in small bowl. Melt butter and chocolate in small saucepan over low heat; set aside. Beat eggs and granulated sugar in large bowl until light. Beat in flour mixture, chocolate mixture, 4 tablespoons Kahlúa, Irish cream and vodka. Fold in walnuts. Pour into greased 13×9-inch baking pan.

Bake in 350°F oven just until toothpick inserted into center comes out clean, about 25 minutes. *Do not overbake.* Cool in pan on wire rack. Spread with Kahlúa Glaze. Decorate with whole coffee beans, if desired. Cut into squares.   *Makes 24 brownies*

KAHLÚA® GLAZE

$1\frac{1}{4}$ cups powdered sugar   3 tablespoons KAHLÚA®

Beat together powdered sugar and 3 tablespoons Kahlúa in small bowl until smooth.

Banana Gingerbread Bars

BANANA GINGERBREAD BARS

1 extra-ripe, medium DOLE®
    Banana, peeled
1 package (14.5 ounces)
    gingerbread cake mix
½ cup lukewarm water
1 egg
1 small DOLE® Banana,
    peeled and chopped
    (½ cup)

½ cup DOLE® Raisins
½ cup DOLE® Slivered
    Almonds
1½ cups powdered sugar
    Juice from 1 DOLE® Lemon

Continued

- Place medium banana in blender. Process until puréed; use ½ cup for recipe.

- Combine gingerbread mix, water, ½ cup puréed banana and egg in large bowl. Beat well.

- Stir in chopped banana, raisins and almonds.

- Spread batter in greased 13×9-inch baking pan. Bake in 350°F oven 20 to 25 minutes until toothpick inserted in center comes out clean.

- Mix powdered sugar and 3 tablespoons lemon juice in medium bowl to make thin glaze. Spread over warm gingerbread. Cool. Cut into bars. Sprinkle with additional powdered sugar if desired.   *Makes 32 bars*

OATMEAL EXTRAVAGANZAS

1 cup all-purpose flour
1½ teaspoons baking powder
½ teaspoon salt
1 cup firmly packed brown sugar
¾ cup (1½ sticks) butter, softened
1 teaspoon vanilla extract

1 egg
2 tablespoons water
2 cups quick oats, uncooked
One 10-ounce package (1½ cups) NESTLÉ® Toll House® Treasures® semi-sweet chocolate deluxe baking pieces

Preheat oven to 375°F. In small bowl, combine flour, baking powder and salt; set aside.

In large mixer bowl, beat brown sugar, butter and vanilla extract until creamy. Beat in egg. Gradually blend in flour mixture, then water. Stir in oats and Nestlé Toll House Treasures semi-sweet chocolate deluxe baking pieces. Spread in greased 9-inch square pan.

Bake 30 to 35 minutes. Cool; cut into 1½-inch squares.

Makes 3 dozen squares

Fanciful Cookies

Beautiful to look at and great-tasting, these cookies take a little extra time to prepare— but they're worth it!

CHOCOLATE-GILDED DANISH SUGAR CONES

½ cup butter or margarine, softened
½ cup sugar
½ cup all-purpose flour
2 egg whites

1 teaspoon vanilla
3 ounces bittersweet chocolate *or* ½ cup semisweet chocolate chips

Preheat oven to 400°F. Generously grease 4 cookie sheets. Beat butter and sugar in large bowl until light and fluffy. Blend in flour. In clean, dry bowl, beat egg whites until frothy. Blend into butter mixture with vanilla.

Using measuring teaspoon, place 4 mounds of dough, 4 inches apart, on each prepared cookie sheet. Spread mounds with back of spoon dipped in water to 3-inch diameter. Bake, 1 sheet at a time, 5 to 6 minutes or until edges are just barely golden. (Do not overbake or cookies become crisp too quickly and are difficult to shape.) Remove from oven and quickly loosen each cookie from cookie sheet with thin spatula. Shape each into a cone; cones become firm as they cool. (If cookies become too firm to shape, return to oven for a few seconds to soften.)

Melt chocolate in small bowl over hot, not boiling, water. Stir until smooth. When all cookies are baked and cooled, dip flared ends into melted chocolate. Let stand until chocolate is set. If desired, serve cones by standing them in a bowl. (Adding about 1 inch of sugar to bottom of bowl may be necessary to hold them upright.)   *Makes 16 cookies*

Chocolate-Gilded Danish Sugar Cones

Orange Pecan Gems

SNOW CAPS

3 egg whites
¼ teaspoon cream of tartar
¾ cup sugar
½ teaspoon vanilla extract
1 cup (6 ounces) semi-sweet
chocolate chips

2 white chocolate baking
bars (2 ounces each),
chopped (optional)

Preheat oven to 200°F. Line baking sheets with parchment paper. In large
mixer bowl, combine egg whites and cream of tartar. Beat at highest
speed of electric mixer until mixture is just frothy. Add sugar, 1
tablespoon at a time, beating well after each addition. Beat until stiff
peaks form. Add vanilla; beat 1 minute. Fold in chocolate chips. Drop
mixture by teaspoonfuls, 1 inch apart, onto prepared baking sheets. Bake
2 hours or until meringues are thoroughly dry to touch but not browned,
rotating baking sheets halfway through baking. Turn off heat. Leave in
closed oven 3 to 4 hours or until completely dry. Remove from oven. Cool
completely. Carefully remove from parchment.

Melt white chocolate in top of double boiler over hot, not boiling, water.
Stir constantly until chocolate melts. Dip top of each cookie into melted
chocolate, if desired. Place on waxed paper to dry. Store at room
temperature in tightly covered containers.

Makes about 6 dozen cookies

ORANGE PECAN GEMS

1 package DUNCAN HINES®
   Moist Deluxe Orange
   Supreme Cake Mix
1 container (8 ounces)
   vanilla lowfat yogurt

1 egg
2 tablespoons butter or
   margarine, softened
1 cup finely chopped pecans
1 cup pecan halves

1. Preheat oven to 350°F. Grease baking sheets.

2. Combine cake mix, yogurt, egg, butter and chopped pecans in large
bowl. Beat at low speed with electric mixer until blended. Drop by
rounded teaspoonfuls 2 inches apart onto greased baking sheets. Press
pecan half onto center of each cookie. Bake at 350°F for 11 to 13 minutes
or until golden brown. Cool 1 minute on baking sheets. Remove to
cooling racks. Cool completely. Store in airtight container.

Makes 4½ to 5 dozen cookies

Tip: Cookies may be stored in an airtight container in freezer for up to 6
months.

HOLIDAY TEATIME TREATS

2 packages (3 ounces each)
   cream cheese, softened
1 cup butter or margarine,
   softened

2 tablespoons sugar
2 cups all-purpose flour

FILLING
½ cup sugar
2 eggs
¼ cup all-purpose flour
1 teaspoon vanilla

1 can SOLO® *or* 1 jar BAKER®
   Apricot or other fruit
   filling
½ cup chopped nuts
   (optional)

Preheat oven to 350°F. Beat cream cheese, butter and 2 tablespoons sugar
in medium bowl with electric mixer until fluffy. Stir in 2 cups flour to
make soft dough. Divide dough in half. Shape each piece of dough into
about 24 (1-inch) balls. Press balls into bottom and up side of ungreased
miniature (1¾-inch) muffin cups. Set aside.

To make filling, beat ½ cup sugar, eggs, ¼ cup flour, vanilla and apricot
filling in medium bowl with electric mixer until blended. Stir in nuts.
Spoon evenly into pastry-lined muffin cups. Bake 25 to 30 minutes or
until filling is set and crust is golden. Cool completely in muffin cups on
wire racks.

Makes about 4 dozen cookies

CHERRY SURPRISES

1 package DUNCAN HINES®
   Golden Sugar Cookie Mix
36 to 40 candied cherries

½ cup semi-sweet chocolate
   chips
1 teaspoon CRISCO®
   Shortening

1. Preheat oven to 375°F. Grease baking sheets.

2. Prepare cookie mix following package directions. Shape thin layer of dough around each candied cherry. Place 2 inches apart on greased baking sheets. Bake at 375°F for 8 minutes or until set but not browned. Cool 1 minute on baking sheets. Remove to cooling racks. Cool completely.

3. Place chocolate chips and shortening in small resealable plastic bag; seal. Place bag in bowl of hot water for several minutes. Dry with paper towel. Knead until blended and chocolate is smooth. Snip pinpoint hole in corner of bag. Drizzle chocolate over cookies. Allow drizzle to set before storing between layers of waxed paper in airtight container.

Makes 3 to 3½ dozen cookies

Tip: Well-drained maraschino cherries may be substituted for candied cherries.

DATE ORANGE COOKIE PIZZA

½ cup margarine, softened
½ cup brown sugar, packed
1 cup all-purpose flour
1 tablespoon orange juice
1 teaspoon grated DOLE®
   Orange peel

1 package (8 ounces) DOLE®
   Pitted Dates, chopped
½ cup DOLE® Almonds,
   toasted and chopped

• Beat margarine and sugar in large bowl until light and fluffy. Gradually beat in flour until blended. Beat in orange juice and peel, then dates and almonds.

• Form dough into ball. Placed on greased 14-inch pizza pan. Pat to 12-inch cookie.

• Bake in 375°F oven 15 minutes. Cool completely. Cut into 14 to 16 wedges to serve.
                              Makes 14 to 16 servings

Cherry Surprises

FLORENTINE CUPS

BASE
- 2 cups HONEY ALMOND DELIGHT® brand cereal, crushed to 1 cup
- 1 cup flaked coconut
- ½ cup raisins
- ½ cup all-purpose flour
- 1½ teaspoons grated fresh orange peel
- ½ teaspoon baking powder
- ½ teaspoon ground cinnamon
- ½ cup packed brown sugar
- ⅓ cup butter or margarine
- ¼ cup honey

ICING
- 1 tablespoon butter or margarine, softened
- ½ cup powdered sugar
- 1½ teaspoons orange juice
- Sliced almonds

To prepare base, preheat oven to 350°F. Grease 32 miniature (1¾-inch) muffin cups. In large bowl, combine cereal, coconut, raisins, flour, orange peel, baking powder and cinnamon; mix well and set aside. In small saucepan, combine brown sugar, ⅓ cup butter and honey. Stir over medium heat until butter is melted and brown sugar is dissolved. Pour over cereal mixture; blend well. Place 1 tablespoon mixture in each prepared muffin cup; press firmly. Bake 8 to 10 minutes or until golden brown (cups will be soft). Cool in pan 15 minutes. Loosen edges. Invert onto wire racks. Cool completely.

To prepare icing, in small bowl, beat 1 tablespoon butter, powdered sugar and orange juice until smooth. With pastry tube, pipe a decorative swirl on top of each cup. Garnish with sliced almonds.

Makes 32 cups

MOCHA MINT CRISPS

- 1 cup butter or margarine, softened
- 1 cup granulated sugar
- 1 egg
- ¼ cup light corn syrup
- ¼ teaspoon peppermint extract
- 1 teaspoon powdered instant coffee
- 1 teaspoon hot water
- 2 cups all-purpose flour
- 6 tablespoons HERSHEY'S Cocoa
- 2 teaspoons baking soda
- ¼ teaspoon salt
- Mocha Mint Sugar (page 83)

Continued

Heat oven to 350°F. In large mixer bowl, beat butter and granulated sugar until light and fluffy. Add egg, corn syrup and peppermint extract; mix thoroughly. Dissolve 1 teaspoon instant coffee in water; stir into butter mixture. Stir together flour, cocoa, baking soda and salt; gradually add to butter mixture, blending thoroughly.

Shape dough into 1-inch balls. (Dough may be refrigerated for a short time for easier handling.) Prepare Mocha Mint Sugar. Roll dough balls in sugar mixture. Place on ungreased cookie sheet, about 2 inches apart. Bake 8 to 10 minutes or until no imprint remains when touched lightly. Cool slightly. Remove from cookie sheet to wire rack. Cool completely.

Makes about 4 dozen cookies

Mocha Mint Sugar: In small bowl, stir together ¼ cup powdered sugar, 2 tablespoons crushed hard peppermint candies (about 6 candies) and 1½ teaspoons powdered instant coffee.

OATMEAL CRANBERRY-NUT COOKIES

¾ cup BUTTER FLAVOR
  CRISCO®
1 cup firmly packed dark
  brown sugar
¼ cup dark molasses
1 egg
2 tablespoons milk
1½ teaspoons vanilla
1 cup all-purpose flour
1¼ teaspoons cinnamon

½ teaspoon baking soda
½ teaspoon salt
¼ teaspoon allspice
1 cup crushed whole-berry
  cranberry sauce
½ cup sliced almonds,
  broken
3 cups quick oats (not
  instant or old
  fashioned), uncooked

1. Heat oven to 375°F. Grease baking sheet with Butter Flavor Crisco.

2. Combine Butter Flavor Crisco and brown sugar in large bowl. Beat at medium speed of electric mixer until well blended. Beat in molasses, egg, milk and vanilla.

3. Combine flour, cinnamon, baking soda, salt and allspice. Mix into creamed mixture at low speed until just blended. Stir in cranberry sauce and nuts. Stir in oats with spoon. Drop tablespoonfuls of dough 2 inches apart onto prepared baking sheet.

4. Bake at 375°F for 12 minutes or until set. Cool 2 minutes on baking sheet. Remove to cooling rack. *Makes about 4 dozen cookies*

CANDY SHOP PIZZA

1½ cups all-purpose flour
½ teaspoon baking soda
½ teaspoon salt
10 tablespoons (1¼ sticks)
    butter, softened
½ cup granulated sugar
½ cup firmly packed brown
    sugar
1 egg
½ teaspoon vanilla extract
One 12-ounce package (2 cups)
    NESTLE® Toll House®
    semi-sweet chocolate
    morsels, divided

½ cup peanut butter
About 1 cup cut-up fruit,
    such as bananas and
    strawberries (optional)
About 1 cup chopped
    candy bars, such as
    NESTLE® CRUNCH® bars,
    BUTTERFINGER® bars,
    ALPINE WHITE® bars,
    GOOBERS® and
    RAISINETS®

Preheat oven to 375°F. In small bowl, combine flour, baking soda and salt; set aside.

In large mixer bowl, beat butter, granulated sugar and brown sugar until creamy. Beat in egg and vanilla extract. Gradually beat in flour mixture. Stir in 1 cup Nestlé Toll House semi-sweet chocolate morsels. Spread batter in lightly greased 12- to 14-inch pizza pan or 15½ × 10½-inch jelly-roll pan. Bake 20 to 24 minutes or until lightly browned.

Immediately sprinkle remaining 1 cup semi-sweet chocolate morsels over crust; drop peanut butter by spoonfuls onto morsels. Let stand 5 minutes or until soft and shiny. Gently spread chocolate and peanut butter over crust. Top with fruit and candy. Cut into wedges. Serve warm.

Makes about 12 servings

Candy Shop Pizza

PARTY!

THE WHOLE CLASS

SCHOOL GYM

PINECONE COOKIES

6 tablespoons butter or
  margarine
1/3 cup HERSHEY'S Cocoa
1 cup sugar
2 eggs
1 teaspoon vanilla extract

2 cups all-purpose flour
1/2 teaspoon baking powder
1/2 teaspoon salt
1/4 teaspoon baking soda
  Light corn syrup
  Sliced almonds

In small saucepan, melt butter over low heat; remove from heat. Add cocoa; blend well. In large mixer bowl, combine sugar, eggs and vanilla; blend in cocoa mixture. Stir together flour, baking powder, salt and baking soda; add to cocoa-sugar mixture, beating until smooth. Refrigerate dough about 1 hour or until firm enough to roll.

Heat oven to 350°F. Roll out small portion of dough between two pieces of waxed paper to 1/8-inch thickness. Cut into pinecone shapes using 2- or 2 1/2-inch oval cookie cutter. Place on lightly greased cookie sheet; lightly brush cookies with corn syrup. Arrange almonds in pinecone fashion; lightly drizzle or brush almonds with corn syrup. Repeat with remaining dough. Bake 7 to 8 minutes or until set. Cool slightly; remove from cookie sheet to wire rack. Cool completely.   *Makes about 4 dozen cookies*

ALMOND-RASPBERRY THUMBPRINT COOKIES

1 cup butter or margarine,
  softened
1 cup sugar
1 can SOLO® *or* 1 jar BAKER®
  Almond Filling
2 egg yolks
1 teaspoon almond extract

2 1/2 cups all-purpose flour
1/2 teaspoon baking powder
1/2 teaspoon salt
1 can SOLO® *or* 1 jar BAKER®
  Raspberry or Strawberry
  Filling

Beat butter and sugar in medium bowl with electric mixer until light and fluffy. Add almond filling, egg yolks and almond extract; beat until blended. Stir in flour, baking powder and salt with wooden spoon to make soft dough. Cover; refrigerate at least 3 hours or overnight.

Preheat oven to 350°F. Shape dough into 1-inch balls. Place on ungreased baking sheets, about 1 1/2 inches apart. Press thumb into center of each ball to make indentation. Spoon 1/2 teaspoon raspberry filling into each indentation. Bake 11 to 13 minutes or until edges of cookies are golden brown. Cool on baking sheets 1 minute. Remove from baking sheets; cool completely on wire racks.   *Makes about 5 dozen cookies*

SPECIAL CHOCOLATE CHIP SANDWICHES

1 package DUNCAN HINES®
    Chocolate Chip
    Cookie Mix
1 egg
2 teaspoons water

8 ounces chocolate-flavored
    candy coating
$\frac{1}{4}$ cup chopped sliced natural
    almonds

1. Preheat oven to 375°F.

2. Combine cookie mix, contents of buttery flavor packet from Mix, egg and water in large bowl. Stir until thoroughly blended. Drop by rounded teaspoonfuls 2 inches apart onto ungreased baking sheets. Bake at 375°F for 8 to 10 minutes or until light golden brown. Cool 1 minute on baking sheets. Remove to cooling racks. Cool completely.

3. Place chocolate candy coating in small saucepan. Melt on low heat, stirring frequently until smooth.

4. To assemble, spread about ½ teaspoon melted coating on bottom of one cookie; top with second cookie. Press together to make sandwiches. Repeat with remaining cookies. Dip one-third of each sandwich cookie in remaining melted coating and sprinkle with almonds. Place on cooling racks until coating is set. Store between layers of waxed paper in airtight containers.
Makes 18 sandwich cookies

Special Chocolate Chip Sandwiches

CHECKERBOARD COOKIES

¾ cup plus 1 tablespoon
   butter or margarine,
   softened and divided
2 egg yolks
½ teaspoon vanilla extract

1 package DUNCAN HINES®
   Moist Deluxe Fudge
   Marble Cake Mix
1 egg, lightly beaten

1. Combine ¾ cup butter, egg yolks and vanilla extract in large bowl. Beat at low speed with electric mixer until blended. Set aside cocoa packet from Mix. Gradually add cake mix. Blend well.

2. Divide dough in half. Add cocoa packet and remaining 1 tablespoon butter to half the dough. Knead until well blended and chocolate colored.

3. Roll out yellow dough between two pieces of waxed paper into a 6-inch square. Repeat with chocolate dough. Remove top pieces of waxed paper from yellow and chocolate doughs. Cut each square into twelve ½-inch-wide strips.

4. To assemble, place one strip chocolate dough on plastic wrap. Brush edge with beaten egg. Place one strip yellow dough next to chocolate dough. Brush edge with egg. Repeat with a second chocolate strip, egg and a second yellow strip to make first row. Brush top of row with egg. Prepare second row by stacking strips on first row, alternating yellow over chocolate strips. Brush edge and top of each strip with egg. Repeat for third row to complete one checkerboard bar. Repeat with remaining strips to make second bar. Cover with plastic wrap. Refrigerate 1 hour or until firm enough to slice.

5. Preheat oven to 350°F. Grease baking sheets.

6. Cut checkerboard bars into ¼-inch slices. Place 2 inches apart on greased baking sheets. Bake at 350°F for 7 to 9 minutes or until edges are light golden brown. Cool 1 minute on baking sheets. Remove to cooling racks. Cool completely. Store in airtight containers.

Makes 4 dozen cookies

DELICATE LACE NUT COOKIES

2 (2-ounce) packages
   PLANTERS® Nut Topping
½ cup firmly packed light
   brown sugar
⅓ cup BLUE BONNET®
   Margarine

3 tablespoons all-purpose
   flour
1 tablespoon milk
1 teaspoon vanilla extract

Continued

Line baking sheets with foil; grease foil. In medium saucepan, combine nut topping, brown sugar, margarine, flour and milk. Cook over low heat, stirring until margarine is melted and mixture is blended. Stir in vanilla; keep warm over low heat. Drop mixture by slightly rounded teaspoonfuls onto prepared baking sheets, about 2½ inches apart.

Bake at 375°F for 4 to 5 minutes or until golden brown. Cool on sheets on wire racks. Carefully peel cooled cookies off foil. Store in airtight containers. *Makes about 4 dozen cookies*

MINIATURE FRUITCAKE JEWELS

FRUITCAKES

1 cup all-purpose flour
⅓ cup BUTTER FLAVOR CRISCO®
⅓ cup granulated sugar
¼ cup orange juice
½ teaspoon baking powder
2 eggs
1 cup diced mixed candied fruit

½ cup quartered red candied cherries
½ cup quartered green candied cherries
1 cup golden raisins
½ cup diced dates
½ cup coarsely chopped pecans

GLAZE

⅓ cup confectioners sugar

2 teaspoons brandy or orange juice

1. Preheat oven to 350°F. Place 22 (2½-inch) foil baking cups in muffin pan cups.

2. **For fruitcakes,** combine flour, Butter Flavor Crisco, granulated sugar, orange juice, baking powder and eggs in large bowl. Beat at low speed of electric mixer until blended. Increase speed to medium. Beat until light and fluffy. Stir in mixed fruit, red and green cherries, raisins, dates and pecans. Spoon into prepared muffin cups, filling about ¾ full.

3. Bake at 350°F for 25 to 27 minutes or until toothpick inserted into center comes out clean. Leave fruitcakes in muffin pans.

4. **For glaze,** combine confectioners sugar and brandy in small bowl. Stir until smooth. Brush lightly over tops of warm baked fruitcakes. Cool in pans. *Makes 22 miniature fruitcakes*

Note: Can also be made in 2-inch baking cups. Place 36 foil baking cups in muffin pan cups. Prepare batter and fill cups as directed in step 2. Bake at 350°F for 18 to 20 minutes or until toothpick inserted into center comes out clean. Makes 36 fruitcakes.

Fancy Walnut Brownies

FANCY WALNUT BROWNIES

BROWNIES
- 1 package DUNCAN HINES®
  Chocolate Lovers' Walnut
  Brownie Mix
- 1 egg

- ⅓ cup water
- ⅓ cup CRISCO® Oil or
  CRISCO® PURITAN® Oil

GLAZE
- 4½ cups confectioners sugar
- ½ cup milk or water

- 24 walnut halves, for garnish

CHOCOLATE DRIZZLE
- ⅓ cup semi-sweet chocolate
  chips

- 1 tablespoon CRISCO®
  Shortening

Continued

1. Preheat oven to 350°F. Place 24 (2-inch) foil liners on baking sheets.

2. **For brownies,** combine brownie mix, egg, water and oil in large bowl. Stir with spoon until well blended, about 50 strokes. Stir in contents of walnut packet from Mix. Fill each foil liner with 2 generous tablespoons batter. Bake at 350°F for 20 to 25 minutes or until set. Cool completely. Remove liners. Turn brownies upside down on cooling racks.

3. **For glaze,** combine confectioners sugar and milk in medium bowl. Blend until smooth. Spoon glaze over first brownie to completely cover. Top immediately with walnut half. Repeat with remaining brownies. Allow glaze to set.

4. **For chocolate drizzle,** place chocolate chips and shortening in small resealable plastic bag; seal. Place bag in bowl of hot water for several minutes. Dry with paper towel. Knead until blended and chocolate is smooth. Snip pinpoint hole in corner of bag. Drizzle chocolate over brownies. Allow chocolate drizzle to set before storing in single layer in airtight containers. *Makes 24 brownies*

CHERRY PINWHEEL SLICES

2 cups all-purpose flour
½ teaspoon salt
1 cup butter or margarine, softened
1 cup dairy sour cream

1 can SOLO® *or* 1 jar BAKER® Cherry, Raspberry or Strawberry Filling
1 cup flaked coconut
1 cup finely chopped pecans Confectioner's sugar

Place flour and salt in medium bowl. Cut in butter until mixture resembles coarse crumbs. Add sour cream; stir until blended. Divide dough into 4 pieces. Wrap each piece separately in plastic wrap or waxed paper; refrigerate 2 to 4 hours.

Preheat oven to 350°F. Roll out dough, 1 piece at a time, on lightly floured surface into 12×6-inch rectangle. Spread one fourth of filling over dough and sprinkle with ¼ cup coconut and ¼ cup pecans. Roll up, jelly-roll style, starting from short side. Pinch seam to seal. Place, seam side down, on ungreased baking sheet. Repeat with remaining dough, filling, coconut and pecans.

Bake 40 to 45 minutes or until rolls are golden brown. Remove from baking sheets to wire racks. Dust liberally with confectioner's sugar while still warm. Cool completely. Cut into 1-inch slices.

Makes about 2 dozen cookies

ACKNOWLEDGMENTS

The publishers would like to thank the companies
and organizations listed below for the use
of their recipes in this publication.

Checkerboard Kitchens, Ralston Purina Company
Dole Food Company, Inc.
Filippo Berio Olive Oil
Hershey Chocolate U.S.A.
Kahlúa Liqueur
Kraft General Foods, Inc.
Nabisco Foods Group
Nestlé Chocolate and Confection Company
The Procter & Gamble Company, Inc.
The Quaker Oats Company
Sokol and Company
Walnut Marketing Board
Wisconsin Milk Marketing Board

PHOTO CREDITS

The publishers would like to thank the companies
and organizations listed below for the use of
their photographs in this publication.

Dole Food Company, Inc.
Hershey Chocolate U.S.A.
Kraft General Foods, Inc.
Nestlé Chocolate and Confection Company
The Procter & Gamble Company, Inc.

Index

METRIC CONVERSION CHART

VOLUME MEASUREMENTS (dry)

$\frac{1}{8}$ teaspoon = 0.5 mL

$\frac{1}{4}$ teaspoon = 1 mL

$\frac{1}{2}$ teaspoon = 2 mL

$\frac{3}{4}$ teaspoon = 4 mL

1 teaspoon = 5 mL

1 tablespoon = 15 mL

2 tablespoons = 30 mL

$\frac{1}{4}$ cup = 60 mL

$\frac{1}{3}$ cup = 75 mL

$\frac{1}{2}$ cup = 125 mL

$\frac{2}{3}$ cup = 150 mL

$\frac{1}{4}$ cup = 175 mL

1 cup = 250 mL

2 cups = 1 pint = 500 mL

3 cups = 750 mL

4 cups = 1 quart = 1 L

VOLUME MEASUREMENTS (fluid)

1 fluid ounce (2 tablespoons) = 30 mL

4 fluid ounces ($\frac{1}{2}$ cup) = 125 mL

8 fluid ounces (1 cup) = 250 mL

12 fluid ounces (1$\frac{1}{2}$ cups) = 375 mL

16 fluid ounces (2 cups) = 500 mL

WEIGHTS (mass)

$\frac{1}{2}$ ounce = 15 g

1 ounce = 30 g

3 ounces = 90 g

4 ounces = 120 g

8 ounces = 225 g

10 ounces = 285 g

12 ounces = 360 g

16 ounces = 1 pound = 450 g

DIMENSIONS

$\frac{1}{16}$ inch = 2 mm

$\frac{1}{8}$ inch = 3 mm

$\frac{1}{4}$ inch = 6 mm

$\frac{1}{2}$ inch = 1.5 cm

$\frac{3}{4}$ inch = 2 cm

1 inch = 2.5 cm

OVEN TEMPERATURES

250°F = 120°C

275°F = 140°C

300°F = 150°C

325°F = 160°C

350°F = 180°C

375°F = 190°C

400°F = 200°C

425°F = 220°C

450°F = 230°C

BAKING PAN SIZES

Utensil	Size in Inches/ Quarts	Metric Volume	Size in Centimeters
Baking or Cake Pan (square or rectangular)	8×8×2	2 L	20×20×5
	9×9×2	2.5 L	22×22×5
	12×8×2	3 L	30×20×5
	13×9×2	3.5 L	33×23×5
Loaf Pan	8×4×3	1.5 L	20×10×7
	9×5×3	2 L	23×13×7
Round Layer Cake Pan	8×1$\frac{1}{2}$	1.2 L	20×4
	9×1$\frac{1}{2}$	1.5 L	23×4
Pie Plate	8×1$\frac{1}{4}$	750 mL	20×3
	9×1$\frac{1}{4}$	1 L	23×3
Baking Dish or Casserole	1 quart	1 L	—
	1$\frac{1}{2}$ quart	1.5 L	—
	2 quart	2 L	—

Fill your home with holiday cheer by baking a batch of delightful *Homemade Holiday Cookies.* Tempt friends and family with scrumptious yuletide favorites like Richest Spritz cookies. Or, make some Miniature Fruitcake Jewels to give as gifts. Celebrate the season with the goodness of fresh-baked cookies, warm from the oven.

ISBN 0-7853-0401-0